"As one who questions my purpose from time to time, Christy's insightful study leads me, and others, to identify the compelling calling God supplanted in me from my very beginnings. If I wondered before about what I'm am created to do, I can say with greater certainty that now I know 'I have to.'

Women — and I believe men too — will welcome a thoughtful progressive study through the question that chases so many throughout life: What am I made to do? By searching for your 'I have to,' Christy helps us let God answer the divine question inside each of us. She also walks us through the costs of pursuing the 'I have to' and the challenges of waiting for the right timing.

Dig deep.. Dream. Discover, and then dive in to what you 'have to' do!"

— Joy Sherman
Pastor, Leader, and Spiritual Director

"Christy Fay is a person deserving of our attention. Her heart for God and desire to see followers of Christ grow in their relationship with Jesus and in their understanding of what God wants to do in and through them produces in her a unique ability walk alongside people in their faith journey. Even more encouraging is that she speaks as one who is engaged in this work each and every day as a pastor at Acadia City Church. We are blessed to have a voice like hers share what God has placed on her heart!"

—Greg Henson
President, Sioux Falls Seminary

"If you are ready to engage your life, some friends, & God, Christy Fay wants to have help you with this pursuit. In this lively study, you have an opportunity to engage the Bible and our Lord in a way that will change your life. Christy is a wonderful conver-ational starter and partner."

—Tom Parker
Director, Fuller Theological Seminary Arizona

I
HAVE
TO

CHRISTY FAY

I

HAVE

TO

chasing

what sets

your soul

on fire

CHRISTY FAY

Carpenter's Son Publishing

I Have To: Chasing What Sets Your Soul on Fire

©2017 by Christy Fay

Published by Carpenter's Son Publishing, Franklin, Tennessee

Published in association with Larry Carpenter of Christian Book Services, LLC
www.christianbookservices.com

Cover Design by Nate Sullivan

Interior Design by Adept Content Solutions

Edited by Robert Irvin

Printed in the United States of America

978-1-945507-01-4

For Michael.

Chasing "I have to's" with you is my
dream come true. Thank you for being
my co-adventurer! I love you.

It's in Christ that we find out who we are and what we are living for.

Ephesians 1:11 (The Message)

CONTENTS

WHAT WAS I
BORN TO DO?

Well hello, friend. I thought you should know how very glad I am that you've found yourself at the beginning of our study. Welcome! I hope you feel at home here as we journey through the Scriptures together over the next six weeks. I know there are so many incredible resources out there for these types of purposes, and that makes me even more humbled to know you've chosen this one!

So let's get right to it, shall we?

I want to address the question you more than likely have bouncing around in your head right now. And actually, it's two questions:

Why did the author write this study?

And: *Why did I pick it up?*

Before I answer that, let me ask a question. If you consider yourself a Christian, if you have turned toward Jesus and invited Him into the center of who you are, then why did you make that choice? Think back to the moment or moments when you gave your life to God. Are you there? OK, good! Now remind yourself of your motivations. What led you to make that kind of commitment?

I wish I could sit down with each and every one of you over a cup of Chai tea (what I'm drinking right now, at this very moment as I type) and listen to your story.

That may not be possible, but we can still journey together! I wonder if any of your answers for coming to Christ had to do with fear, more specifically the fear of a place, a little word we call *h-e-l-l*. You see, for a very long time, to this very day, Christians have often implored a "turn or burn" strategy when attempting to convince others that following God is a good idea. We've asked questions like, "If you were to die tonight, do you know where you're going?" Or, "Where do you want to spend eternity? In the fiery pits of hell, or with the hosts of angels singing and worshiping God?"

In asking these kinds of questions, we've stripped the gospel message of its power and beauty and settled for a kitschy "fire insurance" sales pitch instead.

In doing so, we've led people to believe that God is supremely concerned about where we go when we die and not so much about our quality of life here and now. The Scriptures stand in strict opposition to this thinking, however. Jesus himself declares, "I have come that you might have life and life to the full" (John 10:10). This statement alone seems like proof that God cares deeply about the quality of our lives, here and now, just as much as he cares about where we go when this life is over.

Abundance has been gifted to us by our Creator in many different shapes and sizes: in the extravagant beauty of a sunset or sunrise, or in the way the way the redwoods seem to stretch laboriously up to the heavens, or in the way the waters hitting a beach fold one wave on top of the other, collapsing on the sand below. We uncover life to the full in the warm embrace of our lover, in the cooing of our infants, in the reassuring presence of a parent, and in shared laughter with a friend.

But we also grab hands with this "life to the full" when we uncover that thing we were *made* to do, when we can arrive at the answer to the all-elusive question: "What was I born to do?" and when we can answer it with our hearts full of conviction and certainty. We uncover abundance when we discover our reason for being. Mark Twain summed this up well: "The two most important days in your life are the day you are born and the day you find out why."

It is my greatest hope that this study is a tool in God's hands to unlock your reason for being. Your *"I have to."* Because I believe firmly, with my whole heart, that when we chase after what sets our souls on fire, we are well on our way to a life of abundance. And friends, we must chase ferociously, because Jesus paid a high price for us to have life and have it to the *full.*

As you make your way through this study may you remember, above all, that "God can do anything, you know—far more than you could ever imagine or guess or request in your wildest dreams!" (Ephesians 3:20, *MSG*).

So dream big, dear friends, dream big!

Christy Fay
Scottsdale, Arizona
April 2017

GROUP SESSION GUIDELINES

You may be wondering how in the world you go about facilitating this study in the context of a group setting. This is a great question! So I want to take a minute or two and give you the basics.

1. Decide how often your group is going to meet. Is it once every week or every other week? Either one seems to work great in my experience, so do what works best for your group!

2. When you gather as a group, you will spend time discussing the previous week's homework. (I'm using that term lightly, so don't freak out over it!) You'll find discussion questions at the end of each week of study. Feel free to use this as your guide, but also feel free to pull from any of the content and questions highlighted in the homework that don't appear at the end of a chapter.

3. After you have finished going through the discussion questions, you'll watch a fifteen-minute (give or take a minute or two) video that helps to reinforce and highlight the week's material and content. You'll find these videos at christyfay.com.

Some of you may be wondering what you do the very first week. Again, good question! You will find, below, a few questions to get you started! Feel free to add or subtract as you feel led.

During your initial gathering you will also want to watch the first session. You'll get a chance to meet me and catch a glimpse of where we're going during our six weeks together!

First session question options

1. **When you were little, what did you want to be when you got older?** (Don't hold back; there is no shame in wanting to be in the Ice Capades! Really, there are no wrong answers here.)

2. **What are you doing right now?** (Don't be alarmed if it's not what you thought you would do when you were ten. Few people are doing what they thought they would do when they were ten!)

3. **What's something you are really good at?** (Go ahead: brag about it!)

4. **What's something you absolutely hate doing?** (Go ahead: air it all out.)

5. **What drew you to this study?**

6. **Watch Session 1 at christyfay.com; Introduction.**

Notes, Scribbles, Drawings . . .

At times in our studies you will see blank areas, lines of space for you to write. In those spots, I want you to feel free to write your own notes, draw, or even just scribble. Use your talents; all of this will help you think. Please use these spaces for the things you are thinking and feeling!

Christy

THE SETUP

By the way, you'll be tempted to skip over these parts. How do I know? Because I usually skip over these parts! But if I may be so bold, I urge you: *Read this!* (OK, end of mini sermon.)

I have to. Three little words that seem innocent enough. We speak them aloud perhaps a hundred times a day.

"I have to go to the store."

"I have to take the trash out."

"I have to pay the water bill."

"I have to go to the bathroom."

And all those "I have to's" play a role in our lives. (Especially the bathroom one! It's important to use the restroom when you need to use the restroom; this is something I have been trying to instill in my kids for quite some time!) Anyway, recently, those three little words have taken on deeper a meaning for me. In a sense, I feel like my "I have to" has personified itself and starting slapping me around a bit. I certainly don't feel like I'm in an abusive relationship or anything. It's more like the splash-of-water-in-the-face kind of morning wake-up call that is necessary from time to time to jolt you back into the land of the living.

So what is the "I have to" I am referencing? It's that thing—you know, the *thing*—you daydream about and periodically pantomime when no one is looking. It's the thought in your mind when you wake up, and the thought you can't seem to shake before you drift to sleep. It's that beautiful mixture of passion, obsession, talent, and gift. It's that thing that lights your soul on fire, that thing you can't seem to stop chasing. You can't say no to it, even if you want to, and even though you've tried. It's the one thing you've been given that the world desperately needs. It's your "I have to."

The Japanese—because let's be honest, don't other languages always seem to have more appeal than the one you speak—have a word that sums this up. (On a side note, is there anyone else who's ever dreamt of a child being born to you who utters his or her first words in an adorable British accent? Who cares if you and your husband are from Minnesota. Miracles are possible, right?)

Back to the Japanese. The word they use is *ikigai*. This word is defined as "a reason for being; the thing that gets you up in the morning." Have you ever asked yourself why you're alive?[1] It's a sobering and terrifying question.

If you're experiencing a panic attack right now because you don't know what your "I have to" is, stop, breath, and avoid hyperventilating. First of all, you're in the right place. This Bible study was written to help you discover and live out your "I have to."

Second, it just means you are normal. No one comes out of the womb knowing what they were put on this earth to do. For example, not everyone who operates on their stuffed animals ends up becoming a veterinarian. Not everyone who forced their siblings to do times tables and took great joy in marking F's on top of papers turned out to be teachers. Sometimes we just don't know for a while. And sometimes we think we know and then come to discover we don't.

Sometimes your "I have to" looks like a change in careers or moving your family across the country. It might cause you to leave the workforce and stay at home full time with your children or propel you into foster parenting. Your "I have to" is as unique and original as you are. It is anything from stagnant, and as seasons of your life come and go, your "I have to" morphs and mutates as well.

Yet with all of these variables, one thing will never change. God is the author and creator of all of our "I have to's." There is no *ikigai* without Him. Having wired us Himself, the Scriptures put it this way: He knit us tougher in our mother's womb. He is the key that unlocks every "I have to." So if you're not sure where to start? Pray. Even if you *are* sure where to start: pray.

As we make our way through the next six weeks, commit yourself first to a bended knee and make it a point to consistently cry out to the Maker-God who alone knows the path that lies ahead. The psalmist reminds us that "The LORD makes firm the steps of the one who delights in him" (Psalm 37:23, NIV).

So let's fix our eyes on Him, place our hope in His steadfast faithfulness, and allow Him alone to guide our steps.

---

1 Christopher Peterson, "Ikigai and Mortality," *Psychology Today.* Posted September 17, 2008. Visited September 14, 2015. https://www.psychologytoday.com/blog/the-good-life/200809/ikigai-and-mortality

WHAT IS "I HAVE TO"?"

Day 1: Up on Your Feet!
Jonah 1:1, 2

When I was twelve I met my husband. I just didn't know it at the time! In fact, we did not exchange more than a few words in the next five years. He would tell you it's because of the invisible (or, at times, not-so-invisible) line that divides the popular from the not-so-popular in the world of junior and senior high. He would say I failed to cross that line. I have an alternate version. If you asked me the reason for our lack of communication I would say, "It's his fault." I would say, "I would have crossed that line if he had actually talked to me!"

Regardless of all that, Michael summoned the courage to ask me to homecoming the fall of our senior year, and the rest is history. There isn't a day I'm not thankful for the fact that we have, for all intents and purposes, grown up together. Part of the overlapping of our lives from age seventeen forward means we've shared a home church for the last sixteen years. We attended youth group as high schoolers, chaperoned youth trips as college students, and interned as youth pastors the summer between our junior and senior years. I served as the children's pastor for the first two-and-a-half years of our marriage. We took a year or two break from being on staff before my husband stepped into the role of missions pastor, where he has served for the last four-and-a-half years. McDowell Mountain Church is our home away from home. We are known well, and we know others well. Blood, sweat, and tears have fallen in that place as we have co-labored for the sake of the gospel alongside some of our dearest friends. We have never been more well acquainted with such joy and fulfillment in ministry.

When, about a year and half ago, we sensed God releasing us from our deep ties and connections there, we knew something was up. One night we gathered together as a staff team; the room was vibrating with energy, erupting with all kinds of laughter. Michael and I were filled with such profound love and admiration for every person present, and yet, both separately and collectively, we felt strongly convicted that this season of our lives as part of this staff team was ending.

We realized we were colliding with our "I have to." As the next month unfolded, it became even more clear. God was calling us to plant a new church. We had been blessed beyond measure by McDowell Mountain Church. The church had given us our faith foundation and helped us grow in our journey both personally and in ministry, but now it was time to reproduce. We had been blessed. But we looked at each other, tears in our eyes, with deep assurance. We both knew it: *We have to* go.

* * * * *

As we move forward it will be helpful to have a clear definition in mind for the "I have to" concept we will be using in this study. I outlined this in the introduction. If you haven't done so, please read that short section. You will find the definition, which I stole from the Japanese. Copy it in the space provided below.

Now that we're on the same page, both literally and figuratively, let's jump in. We are going to begin with a man named Jonah. Many of you know his story. The cliffs notes go something like this: God tells Jonah to go to a well-known and influential city, and God has a word from Him to deliver; Jonah goes the other direction; he ends up in the heart of whale's belly before he realizes his no should have been a *yes*. Eventually, he ends up where he was supposed to go, not without a few important lessons along the way. It's the first two sentences of this story I want to dive into today. Read Jonah 1:1,2 below; I've provided it in three different versions.

The word of the Lord came to Jonah son of Amittai: "Go to the great city of Nineveh and preach against it, because its wickedness has come up before me" (Jonah 1:1,2, NIV).

One day long ago, God's Word came to Jonah, Amittai's son: "Up on your feet and on your way to the big city of Nineveh! Preach to them. They're in a bad way and I can't ignore it any longer" (Jonah 1:1,2, MSG).

Now the word of the Lord came unto Jonah the son of Amittai, saying, "Arise, go to Nineveh, that great city, and cry against it; for their wickedness is come up before me" (Jonah 1:1,2, KJV).

Now underline the first few words of verse two. I have done this in the NIV version as an example.

God speaks. And then there is an immediate action step required on Jonah's part. This type of call and response language is repeated over and over again in the Scriptures when we see God interact with prophets and others chosen for His work.

Look up the following references and write the action steps that were required for each of the individuals involved.

Genesis 12:1

Exodus 3:10

Isaiah 6:8, 9

John 5:8

Acts 9:11

God calls and then, in many ways, He forces our hand. There is a crossroads: Either we remain stagnant, unmoved and unstirred, or we *move*. "Arise," "up on your feet," and "go" are the words and phrases used in Jonah 1:1,2. There is little room for argument with God. And so we arrive at the very first step of discovering our "I have to": we must make a move of some kind.

The word *arise* used in the KJV is defined as "the opposite of sitting or kneeling."[2] The definition continues: "It may denote any movement to an erect position." I get the mental image of a parent jolted out of bed by a suspicious thud coming from their infant's room. I can speak from experience: there's nothing like being shocked to attention by the realization that your child has fallen out of their crib. Take a moment and think about a time you experienced this kind of shake-up. Briefly write about that time here.

So I'm wondering: Are you at a crossroads right now? Is there an area of your life God might be calling you to *arise* in? Is it time to "get up on your feet"? If something jumps out to you, write it in the margin. I want acknowledge, though, that this question is not necessarily an easy one to answer. So let's allow the word *Go* in the text to speak to us and broaden our insight on what this might look like in our lives. Examining this concept will help us land on what our action step might be in going forward.

The word for *go* in the original Hebrew language (which Jonah was written in) is *yalak*. Say that one out loud. Kind of rolls off the tongue, doesn't it? The word *yalak* has all kinds of meanings in the English language. I've taken the liberty of writing them out for you below. Read each of these and circle any that apply to your specific circumstances.[3]

Let down	Walk away	Again	Flow
March	Depart	Follow	Bear
Prosper	Go	Lead	Grow
Pursue	Come	Bring	

Phew! That's a lot, isn't it? I hope that one or more of these jumps off the page at you. Now let's answer this: What does *your* yalak look like? You may not be able to determine the entirety of what your *yalak* entails at this exact moment, but let's attempt to put concrete language behind the word or words that you circled. Let me provide an example.

2   James Strong, LLD, STD, *Strong's Expanded Exhaustive Concordance of the Bible* (Nashville: Thomas Nelson, 2010), 6965.

3   James Strong, LLD, STD, *Strong's Expanded Exhaustive Concordance of the Bible* (Nashville: Thomas Nelson, 2010), 3212.

For Michael and me, in the scenario I mentioned at the start of today's study, words like "go," "depart," and "lead" would have been circled and then circled again. And here are some ways we might have put our *yalak* in practical terms:

- *Go* from your home into the land I will show you.
- Step up and *lead* a community that is yet to be formed.
- *Depart* so you can accept the next call in ministry.

So, what does your *yalak* look like? Write, draw, or scribble here!

As we close for today, I want to acknowledge that our *yalaks* may not be easy. It certainly has not been a breeze to leave the church family we had been connected to for the last sixteen years. There have been tears, stress, pain, frustration—and more tears. Changes like these are not always easy, but the premise is that, in spite of the challenges and the pain we might feel because of our *yalak,* it is our "I have to." And so, *we have to.*

Sometimes it's about the fear of where or what God is moving, shoving—or, the gentler way of stating it—calling you toward. For Jonah it was the city of Nineveh.

Look up Nahum 1:14 in the Old Testament. What does it say about Nineveh?

Nineveh is probably the last city that Jonah would have believed to be receptive to the teachings of God; hence, his decision to run in the other direction (Jonah 1:3). Eventually, though, after he spent some time in the belly of the whale, Jonah ended up there, preaching the message of God like he had been asked to do from the start. And, to what must have been his surprise and shock, read what happens in Jonah 3:5.

The Ninevites believed God. A fast was proclaimed, and all of them, from the greatest to the least, put on sackcloth.

What can we learn about God from the repentance of the Ninevites?

Yes. He can do anything. He might be calling us to something or somewhere frightening or unnerving, but He's got a plan, it involves us, and it most definitely involves Him doing far beyond what we could ask or imagine.

So sometimes it's about what God is calling you *toward*. But sometimes it's about what God is asking you to lay down, leave behind, or submit to Him.

The first time we see the word *arise* used in Jonah 1:2 is in Genesis 23:3.

Then Abraham rose from beside his dead wife and spoke to the Hittites. He said, "I am a foreigner and stranger among you. Sell me some property for a burial site here so I can bury my dead."

Abraham's *arise* was connected to the burial of his dear wife Sarai. Sometimes to move forward there are things we must bury. It might be a loss, a certain reputation we have gained, a dream, a relationship, a career, or a preconceived notion of what we thought we would be or who we thought we were. Sometimes our "I have to" means letting go, releasing, and burying.

Perhaps this concept resonates with you. If it does, answer this: What is it that God is asking you to lay down or bury?

This is not an easy way to wrap up today. But we will be spending an entire week of study discussing how to "make room" for our "I have to." Know that I am praying for all of you. May God give us the courage to discover our *yalak*, and may we go after it with all of our hearts.

> **SOMETIMES OUR "I HAVE TO" MEANS LETTING GO, RELEASING, AND BURYING.**

Day 2: Compelled By the Spirit
Acts 20:22–24

Today we land in the book of Acts. You'll notice as we move through our weeks of study together that we will spend time all over the Scriptures—both Old Testament and New Testament. Both are packed with stories that breed insight into our "I have to."

Acts serves as a sort of sequel and was written by the apostle Luke; his first book was quite appropriately called the Gospel of Luke. In Luke's Gospel we meet Jesus, witness His acts, and hear His teaching. In Acts 1:1 Luke reminds the reader of the purpose of his first work: "In my former book, Theophilus, I wrote about all that Jesus began to do and to teach" (Acts 1:1, NIV). If the book of Luke is all about what Jesus began to do, the sequel, Acts, reminds us there is still much to do and accomplish. N. T. Wright, a renowned theologian, remarks that in the book of Acts Jesus "is announced as King and Lord, not as an increasingly distant memory but as a living and powerful reality, a person who can be known and loved, obeyed and followed, a person who continues to act within the real world. We call the book The Acts of the Apostles, but we should think of it as 'The Acts of Jesus (II).'"[4]

The stories in this book are so valuable because the same Jesus of the book of Acts is alive and at work in this present moment in and through the lives of his modern-day apostles—and that's you and me. But we're going to jump into the middle of the story: Acts 20:22–24 will be our focus for today. But first, take a moment to orient yourself with some of the events occurring prior to these verses by beginning your reading in Acts 20:13–24.

Paul is traveling, as he does for the majority of his ministry, from town to town proclaiming the good news that Jesus is the savior of the world. He also spends time following up with and checking in on church communities that are attempting to live out the teachings of Jesus. He has just finished giving some important notes to the elders of the church of Ephesus (Acts 20:17-21) before he launches into a profound statement, one that possesses great meaning for the "I have to" study we are sharing.

"And now, compelled by the Spirit, I am going to Jerusalem, not knowing what will happen to me there" (Acts 20:22).

I'm particularly fascinated by the "compelled by the Spirit" part. Paul is asserting that he has no idea what is going to happen to him, but the bottom line is he "has to" do this. Danger may very well be around the corner, and in fact he has already been warned by the Spirit about impending hardships and persecutions (Acts 20:23), but that in no way

---

4   N.T. Wright, Dale Larsen, Sandy Larsen, *Acts (N.T. Wright for Everyone Bible Study Guides)*, Westminster John Knox Press Louisville, KY, 98–100.

deters him. He is determined. He is steadfast. He is laser-focused. And he is willing to risk it all: "I consider my life worth nothing to me," to accomplish God's mission, he is saying, life worth news of God's grace (20:24). It's inspiring and, at the same time, conjures up a certain amount of conviction—or a lot of conviction, if I'm honest.

What strikes you most about Paul's character in light of his mission? Journal your thoughts here.

Let's dig deeper into this whole concept of being compelled. The word in the Greek is *deo*, and its English equivalent is *bound*. It's defined as "to bind, to tie, to be fastened, fastened with chains." So Paul is compelled, tied, or chained to go to Jerusalem, much like he was literally handcuffed and chained while in prison (Acts 16:22–24). So often there is a negative connotation involved with being chained or shackled. We don't love the idea of being at the mercy and whim of someone else. We don't want to be shackled by anyone or anything! But when the word "compelled" is followed by the words "by the Spirit," an entirely different picture is painted. Paul's compulsion to preach the good news is a life-altering shackling, and I'm not speaking of just his own. Millions were forever changed because of his "I have to."

So, let's get practical. Is there anything you feel compelled to do? The kind of *compelled* that chains or ties you to something by the power of the Spirit?

As you consider this question—and perhaps you are feeling a bit stumped—let me pose another one! What is something you are consistently drawn to? Almost like the north side is drawn to the south side of a magnet, what captivates and enraptures you? What pulls you in, not just once but over and over again? If we can take the time to pinpoint those passions, activities, and exercises that tug on our hearts and resonate deeply in our souls, we are getting much closer to our "I have to." Parker Palmer wrote about the importance of listening to your life's passion in his book *Let Your Life Speak: Listening for the Voice of Vocation*. Palmer writes, "Before you tell your life what you intend to do with it, listen for what it intends to do with you. Before you tell your life what truths and values you have decided to live up to, let your life tell you what truths you embody, what values you represent."[5]

For me it's writing and teaching, which I am doing now. As a child, I distinctly remember the joy associated with propping my take-home folder upright on my desk, a blank page in front of me, a pencil perched between by index finger and thumb. I was in fourth grade, but I remember it like it was yesterday.

And other, similar times: my speech class in high school, being chosen as the first student ever to preach to my peers in my college group's weekly gathering, receiving a degree in education, an invitation to join my home church preaching team—these were all road

SO, LET'S GET PRACTICAL. IS THERE ANYTHING YOU FEEL COMPELLED TO DO? THE KIND OF *COMPELLED* THAT CHAINS OR TIES YOU TO SOMETHING BY THE POWER OF THE SPIRIT?

signs for me, markers along the way. Each signpost led me to this. I was made to write and teach. I love it. I wake up thinking about it and go to sleep dreaming of it. I am drawn in again and again. The many opportunities that have surfaced to live out these two activities over the course of the last fifteen years have served to confirm this passion in my life. Writing and teaching are distinct, undeniable parts of my "I have to."

I invite you to participate in a short exercise. I believe it will be especially helpful if you're having a hard time conceptualizing your "I have to." Begin with prayer. Ask God to bring to the forefront of your mind experiences, important moments, from your past. Then reflect on and journal what God has brought to mind from the following periods of time.

Early childhood/elementary years:

Junior and senior high years:

5 Parker J. Palmer, *Let Your Life Speak: Listening for the Voice of Vocation*, Jossey-Bass, San Francisco, CA 2000 65–67.

College and early career:

Early career to the present moment:

For Christ's love compels us, because we are convinced that one died for all, and therefore all died (2 Corinthians 5:14).

To close today, answer one last question.
What is Christ's love compelling you to do *today*? Write or draw your thoughts here.

Day 3: The Gift You Give the World
Ephesians 4:1–13

I so wish I could sit across the table from you and hear what yesterday's lesson stirred up, what rose to the surface. It is so good to just pause, reflect, and glance over our own shoulder to see where life has been leading us and what it might be telling us about our future, isn't it? What seemed like mere coincidence, activities, and opportunities we merely stumbled upon are actually critical steps on our journey, ones planned and purposed by our Creator. We are here in this moment, standing on the precipice of what's to come, because of what *has* come.

A part of Paul's journey was the subject of yesterday's lesson, and this is true for today's lesson as well. However, for today, we will land in a book written by Paul himself and addressed to the church at Ephesus. We will pick up in chapter four. (No, I am not asking you to read all three of the previous chapters!) But it might be helpful to know, as we enter the text, that Paul has spent the first three chapters focused on describing a new society that has and is being formed by the work of Christ, his death, and his resurrection. Then, writes John Stott, the "apostle moves on from the new society to the new standards which are expected of it."[6] There are several standards which Paul lays out in chapter four, Stott writes, the charity of our character, the unity of our God, the diversity of our gifts, and the maturity of our growth.[7] We will focus on the third standard, the diversity of our gifts, but for now, write the first six words of Ephesians 4:1 in the space below.

Yesterday we talked about the idea of being bound to a calling in the same way we might be physically shackled to something. I love how Paul begins this chapter, because he reminds us that above all He is bound to the Lord. Stott writes, "He (Paul) again describes himself as a prisoner for the Lord, using a slightly different grammatical construction but the same double entendre, that he is both a prisoner of Christ and a prisoner for Christ, both bound to him by the chains of love and in custody out of loyalty to his gospel."[8]

Paul goes on to write, "I urge you to live a life worthy of the calling you have received" (Ephesians 4:1, NIV). Or another way of describing this might be to live out your

---

6   John Stott, *The Message of Ephesians: The Bible Speaks Today Series* (InterVarsity Press: Kindle Edition). April 2, 2014.

7   Ibid.

8   Ibid.

"heavenly destiny," as James Strong writes.[9] That is a stunning sentiment; I love the pairing of these two words! But what exactly do they mean? Of course, Paul is already ahead of us. According to the great apostle, it looks like this: humility, patience, forbearance, unity and, most important for us today, the exercising of our gifts given to us by Christ himself (see Ephesians 4:2–7).

Fill in the blank:

But to each one of us _____ has been given as Christ apportioned it (Ephesians 4:7).

What does it mean that grace has been given to us? Great question. The word "grace" in the Greek is *charis*, and it is defined as "the divine influence upon the heart, and its reflection in the life."[10] God works in us and then calls us to give Him the space to work though us.[11] In other words, he gifts us with his presence so we might be a gift to the world.

Read the remainder of Ephesians 4:7 if you haven't already done so. Are you as dumbfounded as I was? What exactly does Paul mean that "he ascended on high, he took many captives, and gave gifts to the people"? It's important to note that he is using the language from Psalm 68:18:

When you ascended on high,

you took many captives;

you received gifts from people,

even from the rebellious—

that you, Lord God, might dwell there.

Notice that the wording from the psalm and Paul's wording in Ephesians 4:7 is exceptionally similar, with one distinct difference. In the Psalm 68 the subject (the conqueror) receives gifts while in Paul's context the subject (God) *gives* gifts. Most scholars believe this is no mishap on Paul's part. The psalm describes a king who has just conquered new territory and is returning to his home city. He is ascending on high, walking the uphill path of Mount Zion, which leads to the holy city, Jerusalem. He forces his captives to march in a line behind him, on parade for all to see. The gifts that are received by the king are the booty, the loot that has been taken from the conquered city. These gifts are then distributed to his people.

---

9   James Strong, LLD, STD, *Strong's Expanded Exhaustive Concordance of the Bible* (Nashville: Thomas Nelson, 2010), 2821.

10 Ibid, 5485.

11 William Barclay, *The Letters to the Galatians and Ephesians (The New Daily Study Bible)* (Louisville, Kentucky: Westminister John Knox Press, 2002), 165.

Stay with me; here's where it gets good. Paul has used what would be a very familiar scenario to his audience, and he has put it within the context and work of Christ. Jesus ascended on high, joining the Father in Heaven. "His train of captives being the principalities and powers he had defeated, dethroned and disarmed,"[12] as John Stott puts it. Jesus, then, instead of receiving gifts for himself, *gives* all kinds of gifts, supremely the Holy Spirit, who then leads and guides us into the God-given work we are called to.

This is a tricky theological package to unwrap. But if we do so carefully, there is much to behold. Christ has taken away anything that would set itself up in opposition to us as we attempt to live out our callings, exercising the gifts we have been given. What kinds of powers has Christ defeated, dethroned, and disarmed? As you answer that, think about the kinds of things that hold you back from chasing your "I have to's."

Fear, laziness, lack of confidence, mistrust, and anything else you named in the blank above has no power over us—unless we let it. These things have been defeated, but we have to live as conquerors, not as those who have been conquered. That choice lies in our hands and in ours alone.

So if He has given us gifts, what do they look like, and what is their purpose? Paul answers these questions for us. Go on and read Ephesians 4:9–13. What are some of the specific gifts Paul describes in these verses?

We could spend a great deal of time diving into each of these. Of course, it would only begin to scratch the surface of the many different gifts outlined in other sections of Scripture, and we still would not begin to cover the vast number of remaining gifts not mentioned. Instead, I want to focus our attention on why we receive these gifts, which Christ worked so hard to distribute to us through His Spirit.

According to Ephesians 4:12, 13 why are we given gifts?

Verse twelve in the King James Version reads, "For the perfecting of the saints, for the work of the ministry, for the edifying of the body of Christ." Over the years, because of the use of the word "ministry," people have assumed that Paul is talking specifically about gifts given to those in vocational ministry. It's assumed, then, that pastors, priests, and others within vocational ministry are alone responsible for the building up of the body and the maturity either attained to or not by their flock or congregation. Although this is partially true, it is far from the whole picture. John Stott writes, "For the word ministry (*diakonia*) is here used not to describe the work of pastors but rather the work

12 Stott, *The Message of Ephesians* (InterVarsity Press: Kindle Edition), April 2, 2014.

of so-called laity, that is, of all God's people without exception."[13] We have all been given grace, gifts distributed to each of us that are meant to bless the world. Not only will we suffer if we hold these gifts close and fail to release them, more than anything, the body of Christ suffers. It is no coincidence that Paul uses the image of a body when describing the importance of each and every gift to the functioning of the whole.

Even so, the body is not made up of one part but of many. "Now if the foot should say, 'Because I am not a hand, I do not belong to the body,' it would not for that reason stop being part of the body. And if the ear should say, 'Because I am not an eye, I do not belong to the body,' it would not for that reason stop being part of the body. If the whole body were an eye, where would the sense of hearing be? If the whole body were an ear, where would the sense of smell be? But in fact God has placed the parts in the body, every one of them, just as he wanted them to be" (1 Corinthians 12:13–18).

Every gift is important and every gift is meant to edify. Once again, Stott has some great insight for us: "All spiritual gifts, then, are service-gifts. This is their purpose. They are not given for selfish but for unselfish use, namely for the service of other people."[14] Jesus lays does his life that we might find ours, and in turn lay down ours for the sake of others. This is how the message of Jesus is reproduced in the world. It is no small task to dis-

FEAR, LAZINESS, LACK OF CONFIDENCE, MISTRUST, AND ANYTHING ELSE YOU NAMED IN THE BLANK ABOVE HAS NO POWER OVER US—UNLESS WE LET IT. THESE THINGS HAVE BEEN DEFEATED, BUT WE HAVE TO LIVE AS CONQUERORS.

cover what we were put on this earth to do, but finding it and putting it into practice not only changes us, it changes the world.

I love how this was put by actor and comedian Jim Carrey. If you haven't watched his commencement speech to the graduates of Maharishi University, you should. He talks about all kinds of things, from a bit about his upbringing to how he found his calling to how to bridle your creativity. He says, at one point in his inspiring speech, "The effect you have on others is the most valuable currency there is." I found it fascinating that a man with so much money and undeniable success would assert that the greatest thing

13 John Stott, *The Message of Ephesians:* The Bible Speaks Today Series (InterVarsity Press: Kindle Edition). April 2, 2014.

14 John Stott, *The Message of Ephesians:* The Bible Speaks Today Series (InterVarsity Press: Kindle Edition). April 2, 2014.

you can do for others is find out what you were made to do—and then give it away. I want to close with a question that I stole from Jim (I'm now talking about him like he's a friend!).

"How will you serve the world? What do they need that your talent [I (Christy) would insert: *gift*] can provide?"[15]

Watch Session 1 at Christyfay.com: Introducing "I Have To."

---

15 Jim Carrey, Commencement Address, speech presented at Maharishi University of Management, Fairfield, IA, May 2014.

Day 4: Search My Heart
2 Samuel 15:1–12

I have three handsome boys. And I love each of their names: Oliver Moses, Wesley Jack, and Crosby Sawyer. I am biased, but those are some great names! When I was pregnant with our fourth, we realized we had made a big mistake. We had used every single boy name that existed that we loved! Michael asked me one night, "Do you think we could just use of the boys' middle names if we have another son?" "No," I responded. "Surely we can think of one more name we like." But we couldn't. We went through lists and lists. Popular boy names from the 1950s, rock star boy names, top ten celebrity boy names. Nothing. It was easy to eliminate them from our list, but picking the right one seemed like a nearly impossible task. Luckily for us, we had a girl, and we happily used the name we had chosen for her and had never been able to use in the eight years since the birth of our first.

My point here is sometimes it's easier to decide what you don't like before you settle on what you do. When attempting to define what "I have to" is, it can be beneficial to see what "I have to" is *not*.

From today's Scripture, our friend Absalom models what not to do in terms of his "I have to," helping us figure out what not to do in terms of ours. The name Absalom may ring a bell for you, or it may not. Let's find out a little bit more about him before we land in 2 Samuel 15 for the remainder of today. Answer the following questions by looking up the Scripture reference provided.

Who was Absalom's father? (2 Samuel 3:3)

What happens to Absalom's sister? (1 Samuel 13:1–21)

How does Absalom react to what happened to his sister? (1 Samuel 13:28–29)

After the murder of Amnon, Absalom flees, seeking refuge under the King of Geshur. He spends three years in a foreign land before he makes his way back to Jerusalem. You might think time brings some form of remorse to Absalom and perhaps an aspiration to reconcile with his father David. This is not the case. It seems, if anything, that time has only served to ignite and foster Absalom's desire for revenge. Perhaps he believes David is responsible in some way for the rape of his sister. After all, if the king had not sent for Tamar to join Amnon on his "sick bed," this all could have been avoided. Regardless of Absalom's true motivations, it is quite clear he is dead set on enacting a coup. And that is where we pick up our story. Read 2 Samuel 15:1-12.

Let's break down this maniacal plot for revenge. Fill in the blanks below after studying 2 Samuel 15:1–5 (the following will use the NIV version).[16]

Step 1: Puffing up his reputation
In the course of time, Absalom provided himself with a _____ and horses and fifty men to _____ ahead of him (2 Samuel 15:1).

Step 2: Strategic position
He would get up early and stand by the side of the road leading to the _____ gate (2 Samuel 15:2).

Step 3: Taking advantage of the people's vulnerabilities
Whenever anyone came with a _____ to be placed before the king for a decision, Absalom would _____ out to him (2 Samuel 15:2).

Step 4: Discrediting his superior
Then Absalom would say to him, "Look, your claims are valid and proper, but there is no _____ of the king to hear you" (2 Samuel 15:3).

Step 5: Exalting his own abilities
And Absalom would add, "If only I were appointed judge of the land! Then everyone who has a complaint or case could come to _____ and see that they receive _____" (2 Samuel 15:4).

Step 6: Playing to their emotions
Also, whenever anyone approached him to bow down before him, Absalom would reach out his hand, take hold of him, and _____ him (2 Samuel 15:5).

Although it's completely devious, you have to admit it's equally brilliant. As I wrote this, we were in the midst of a year of presidential elections, and I found myself sincerely

---

16 David Guzik, *Verse by Verse Commentary 2 Samuel* (Santa Barbara, California: Enduring Word Media, 2012).

wondering if some of the candidates on either side of the political aisle had pulled a page from Absalom's book. I'm sure glad we have no men and women these days on the election trail looking to glorify themselves and play to the emotions of the people in order to advance their careers!

I think verse six adds more fuel to the fire of Absalom's already shady motives. "Absalom behaved this way toward all the Israelites who came to the king asking for justice, and so he stole the hearts of the people" (2 Samuel 15:6). The word *stole* is interesting because it inherently asserts the hearts of the people aren't Absalom's to claim. David is still ruling, and any attempt to undermine his authority is flat-out wrong; in fact, it's treasonous.

If you can believe it, things get even more tasteless and heinous; Absalom takes things a step further. Although his desire to go "worship" at Hebron (2 Samuel 15:7) seems honorable at first, in reality it has nothing to do with God-worship and everything to do with Absalom-worship.

THIS CAN AND SHOULD BE A LESSON TO US. OUR "I HAVE TO" SHOULD ORIGINATE WITH GOD AND BE ENABLED BY HIM.

He is about to drive in the ground the final stake of his plot to claim the throne, and it's all going down in Hebron. Absalom earns the approval of his father for this sojourn. David remarks, "Go in peace." Of course, peace is the last thing on Absalom's mind, and he is willing to evoke—even corruptly so—the name of the Lord in order to carry out his plan.[17]

This can and should be a lesson to us. Our "I have to" should originate with God and be enabled by Him. If you have to lie, coerce, manipulate, demoralize, and sabotage in order to make your "I have to" come to fruition, it's a clear red flag. It is clearly not God's vision or mandate for Absalom to be king; it is Absalom's own. His steps are not laid out and marked by God but calculated and orchestrated by himself.

By contrast, in Joshua chapter one, Joshua is given the final go-ahead by God to cross the Jordan and lay hold of the land God has promised the Israelites. There is one thing in particular God communicates to Joshua on that day—thousands of years ago—that holds great relevance for us, today, as we pursue and discover our individual "I have to." Read Joshua 1:2,3.

"Moses my servant is dead. Now then, you and all these people, get ready to cross the Jordan River into the land I am about to give to them——to the Israelites. I will give you every place where you set your foot, as I promised Moses."

---

17   David Guzik, *Verse by Verse Commentary 2 Samuel* (Santa Barbara, California: Enduring Word Media, 2012).

The steps we take on the journey of our "I have to" should not be contrived and forged by ourselves, but by God. He will give us every place we set our feet. Of course, this only applies if we are moving toward the land He has promised us. Absalom has never been promised kingship, and so any knees bowed to him, any hearts turned, and any allegiance gained is not because of God's favor or sovereignty. Eventually, we will see that Absalom's ruse lasts only a short time. When our plans belong to us and not the Lord, ruin is the ultimate destination, and our true motivations will be sifted to the surface.

Job 5:12 says, "He thwarts the plans of the crafty, so that their hands achieve no success."

This principle is surely true in the life of Absalom, and it will be true in ours as well.

Important note: today's lesson was not meant to conjure up conviction and guilt where there need not be! If you are confident your "I have to" comes from the Lord and your motives are pure, you can proceed with boldness and confidence, trusting Him to give you every place you set your foot.

As I write this, my first Bible study has just been released. If I'm honest, I want it to sell, and preferably lots of copies. And I have to ask myself, and take a candid survey: Is the root of that desire for God t message to be glorified or for the glory of the messenger? I think the answer vacillates, which is not something I'm too proud of. But it's the truth.

Take the next few minutes to pray. Perhaps you will want to begin with Psalm 139:23: *"Search me God, and know my heart; test me and know my anxious thoughts."*

Ask Him to sift, sort, and pluck out selfish motives. Give Him space to fine-tune and recalibrate your heart to make it more like His. As you pray, write what surfaces below.

Day 5: In Spite Of
2 Samuel 15:21

Yesterday we closed with a time of prayer and reflection. I hope you took few minutes to allow God to search and know your heart (Psalm 139:23). Today we're going to pick up where we left off in the story of Absalom and his plot to overthrow David's rule. We ended yesterday with Absalom's trip to Hebron, which, at first glance, appeared noble. Instead, it was actually rooted in deceit. Let's pick up the story at 2 Samuel 15:10–14.

How many men accompanied Absalom to Jerusalem?

Who else does Absalom send for?

2 Samuel 15:12 tells us Ahithophel the Gilonite is David's counselor. Although this text does not elaborate further on the relationship between Ahithophel and David, we gain great insight into the quality and depth of their relationship in Psalm 41. Turn to Psalm 41:9. What words does David use to describe this moment of betrayal?

We can all agree things aren't going well for David. His son Absalom is on a rampage of revenge and will stop at nothing until the throne has been overturned (insert knife directly in back). One of his closest friends and advisors has now turned his back on him (twist knife). David has lost the trust and devotion of his people and is subsequently forced out of his own home (twist knife again).

Have you ever experienced a betrayal like this? Where the ones closest to you have turned their backs and left you feeling defeated and utterly alone? Perhaps you can identify with being forced to flee from your own home because you feared for your safety.

Unfortunately, we can probably all identify with David in some way. Very few of us escape life without some kind of betrayal, defeat, and abandonment. Luckily for David, one man changes the trajectory of the situation. We are about to meet Ittai the Gittite. (Say that three times over; it's actually pretty fun to do so!) In this dark day for David, Ittai will become a beacon of hope for the king, a "bright spot in this dark story."[18]

Read 2 Samuel 15:15-22.

David watches as his personal bodyguard and six hundred Gittites (those who had remained loyal to him from his time spent in Gath[19]) march past him on their way out of the city. That's a long line of people, and it provides David ample time to reflect on the misery of his circumstances. His family has deserted him, and his closest friends have sided with his enemy—his own son. "My heart is in anguish within me; the terrors of death have fallen on me. Fear and trembling have beset me; horror has overwhelmed me" (Psalm 55:4). David would record these words later while reflecting on this particular moment in time.

But Ittai enters, and the tide begins to turn, ever so subtly. Strangely enough, David does his best to dissuade Ittai from following him. Fill in the blanks with the arguments David uses to convince Ittai he is making the wrong choice by committing to follow him (2 Samuel 15:19, 20).

1). You are a _____.

2). An exile from your _____.

3) You came only _____.

4) And today I shall make you wander about with us, when I do not _____ where I am going

5) Go _____, and take your people with you. May the Lord show you kindness and faithfulness.

These are some pretty valid points if you ask me, but Ittai nonetheless pushes back. His reply gives us all kinds of insight into what our "I have to" should look like. Write Ittai's response (2 Samuel 15:21) in the space below.

18 Eugene H. Peterson, *First and Second Samuel (Westminster Bible Companion)* (Presbyterian Publishing Corporation), Kindle Edition.

19 David Guzik, *Verse by Verse Commentary 2 Samuel* (Santa Barbara, California: Enduring Word Media, 2012).

This is the climax of the story. It's the defining moment. David has given up hope. He excuses Ittai from any obligation he might feel to stand by him. I can only imagine that David is assuming, after this short speech, that Ittai will turn and walk away, joining the ranks of Absalom like everyone else. "The foreigner, however, expresses passionate loyalty to and solidarity with David, promising to stay with David in every circumstance" (v. 21). David Guzik writes, "We can learn a lot from Ittai's demonstration of loyalty."[20]

Ittai did it when David was down.

> Ittai did it decisively.
>
> Ittai did it voluntarily.
>
> Ittai did it having newly come to David.
>
> Ittai did it publicly.
>
> Ittai did it knowing that the fate of David became his fate."[21]

Ittai remains true to his convictions in spite of the many and varied reasons to turn away. His determined commitment to his "I have to" can teach us all lessons about what our "I have to" should look like. Because the thing about our "I have to" is it's not going to be easy. It wasn't for Ittai, and it won't be for us. It's going to require the kind of resolve that Ittai exhibits. Your "I have to" might involve quitting a job, leaving an abusive relationship, or staying in a marriage that feels irreparable. Perhaps it looks like quitting a job or moving across the country. It might look like adopting a child or becoming foster parents. For us, it meant leaving a church we had called home for sixteen years in order to multiply God's kingdom beyond our comfort zone.

ITTAI REMAINS TRUE TO HIS CONVICTIONS IN SPITE OF THE MANY AND VARIED REASONS TO TURN AWAY. HIS DETERMINED COMMITMENT TO HIS "I HAVE TO" CAN TEACH US ALL LESSONS.

The bottom line is there will be challenges, obstacles, and plenty of reasons not to do what we are feeling otherwise compelled to do. Our "I have to" may force us to move against the grain of culture. David was not the popular choice, but Ittai followed him anyway.

---

20 Walter Brueggemann, *First and Second Samuel: Interpretation: A Bible Commentary for Teaching and Preaching* (Presbyterian Publishing Corporation). Kindle Edition.

21 David Guzik, *Verse by Verse Commentary: Genesis* (Santa Barbara, California: Enduring Word Media, 2012).

We must be decisive. We must submit ourselves to the Lord and trust that he will lead us to places of greater purpose and depth of meaning. If you are new to your journey of faith, Ittai reminds us that this is no excuse; we should delve deeper and march on. We don't shy away or shrink back; we stand firm, resolved to do what we have to do. There may be persecutions, or our closest friends and family may question our decisions, but we forge ahead regardless.

Which of the characteristics of Ittai's loyalty resonates with you most? Why?

As we wrap us this week, I hope your "I have to" is beginning to form and make its way to the surface. Don't worry! It's just week one; we still have lots of work to do. We are only inching toward the preverbal cliff; you don't have to be ready to jump yet! That's coming, though. So get ready.

I care about each of you. I can't tell you how badly I want for you to live into your true God-ordained potential. Each and every one of you is a gift, and I am so humbled be on this journey with you.

MAKING SPACE FOR "I HAVE TO"

The Setup

A few months ago, I lost my mind. OK, not literally. But I read a book by Marie Kondo called *The Life-Changing Magic of Tidying Up*. This is a must read. Especially if you've ever felt like the "stuff" in your house (like that book you read fifteen years ago but can't let go of, or the dress you wore for the wedding that is now 4 sizes too small, or the extra toaster you keep around in case yours breaks) has stolen control and, with it, destroyed the quality of your life. What I mean by that is you are buried, literally or figuratively, under a pile of seemingly necessary items that you can't seem to part with no matter how hard you try. Meanwhile, you can't seem to shake the feeling that you are being suffocated, but when you look around to find the culprit, there is no one there. Have you ever felt claustrophobic in your own home? Maybe because every nook and cranny is filled with some kind of inanimate object that somehow convinces you, with its sad little nonexistent eyes, that it must stay. Said item is now driving the wheel of your emotions, and in its fully personified form has persuaded you that kicking it to the curb will scar it for life.

In case you haven't caught on yet, I'm speaking from experience. I've felt all of that! I'm not a hoarder. At least, I don't think I am. But I have found myself enslaved by my "stuff."

Kondo's book gives some practical, even revolutionary tips on how to part with items that take up space, and it begins doing so by asking one simple question: does this item

25

evoke any sense of joy? If it does, it stays. If it doesn't, it goes. Kondo urges her clients and readers to first discard everything that doesn't spark joy. Then, and only then, she directs, can you begin to find a proper home (i.e., space) for the keepers. She insists that if you follow these instructions—discard first and then sort and put away—you will discover that everything has a place.[22]

I didn't buy what she was selling—at first. But I'm telling you, it's true. And I think it's true for more than just monetary items. I'm now convinced that we can't fully embrace our "I have to" until we have made space for it first. What do I mean by that? Great question. I'm positive I cannot say it any better than Elle Luna did, in her brilliant book *The Crossroads of Should and Must*. There is nothing that distracts or pollutes our "musts"—or to put it in our terminology, our "I have to's"—more than our "shoulds" or our "I want to's."[23]

So we have to do some housekeeping. We have to clean out our "I want to's" and dust away those "shoulds" so there is space for our "musts" and "I have to's." The problem is sometimes we don't even realize we are living in the land of "I want to's" and "shoulds." And perhaps, even more than that, the land seems plenty good to us. And you have probably heard this famous truth: the most dangerous enemy of *great* is *good*. We aren't always aware that there is a voice in our head that isn't ours, and certainly isn't God's, a voice that keeps us from the abundant life we were intended to live.

Here's how this plays out scientifically. We have a conscious mind and a subconscious mind. Our conscious minds are controlled by the frontal lobe of our brains. It is this sector of our brain that is responsible for the processing of all information. It controls things like worry, reasoning, math facts, and the name of the person we just met. So you can blame your conscious mind when you whisper to someone, maybe your spouse or a friend next to you: "Was her name Sally or Sarah? Or was it Cynthia? Ugh. I can't remember."

Here's where it gets interesting. It is the conscious part of our brains that doesn't develop until we hit puberty. Which immediately makes me wonder: what in the world did I use to think with in the first twelve or more years of my life? The answer? The subconscious mind. It is all about feelings and perceptions. It is where all outside information is stored and processed.[24]

Author Jen Sincero writes, "Our subconscious mind, on the other hand, is the non-analytical part of our brain that's fully developed the moment we arrive here on earth. . . . The subconscious mind believes everything because it has no filter, it doesn't know the difference between what's true and what's not true. If our parents tell us that nobody in our family knows how to make money, we believe them. If they show us that marriage

22 Marie Kondo, *The Life-Changing Magic of Tidying Up* (Berkley, California: Ten Speed Press, 2015).

23 Elle Luna, *The Crossroads of Should and Must* (New York: Workman Publishing Co., 2015).

24 Jen Sincero, *You Are a Badass* (Philadelphia: Running Press Book Publishers, 2013), 19–20.

means punching each other in the face, we believe them. We believe them when they tell us that some fat guy in a red suit is going to climb down the chimney and brings us presents—why wouldn't we believe any of the other garbage they feed us?"[25]

Right about now, you're thinking: Well, that's good and fine. There are two parts of our minds: the conscious and the subconscious. What's wrong with that?

And the answer is: nothing. Except the fact that most of the time we believe our conscious minds are in control, that this side is the one dominating the conversation. Meanwhile, our subconscious is lounging around in the sofa of our brains eating a bag of chips and laughing maniacally because it's the one actually holding the reigns of our thought life and therefore our actions.

Our conscious minds say: "Yes. Go for it. Open your own business! Ask that girl out! Quit your job and travel for a year!" And your subconscious mind very quietly goes about the business of pulling all sorts of memories to the forefront, most of which you were sure you had erased. Like that one involving the chubby and insecure kid in third grade who picked on you and made you feel you were good for nothing. And before you know it, your subconscious mind has deterred you from your "I have to" and left you curled up in the old, worn-in, and all-too-comfortable recliner that is your "I want to." Am I talking to anyone else here except myself?

So there you have it. Our "should" versus our "must." Our "I want to" versus our "I have to." And our conscious versus our subconscious. All these battles going on in our hearts and brains can leave us feeling—well—a bit confused and overwhelmed. Now we know why we feel so scattered, unsure, and discontent half of the time. Or maybe, in reality, more than half of the time.

The questions we will be examining this week are: Now what? How do we make space? How do we push the reset button? How do we let go and let God? How do we release the "I want to" to make a way for the "I have to"?

First,

Day 1

1. What kind of call and response language does God use with Jonah? What about the other references you looked up? What kinds of actions steps were required of these individuals?

2. What does your *yalak* look like right now?

---

25 Ibid.

Day 2

1. Is there anything you feel *compelled* to do? The kind of compelled that chains or ties you to something by the power of the Spirit?

   hanging out /encouraging the elderly

2. As you participated in the exercise for this day, were there activities or experiences you were drawn to again and again? If so, what were they? How can this help you as you wrestle with your "I have to"?

Day 3

1. What kinds of things are holding you back from chasing your "I have to"? What does it mean to live life as a conqueror, not as one who has been conquered?

   fear of failure.

2. How will you serve the world? What do people need that only your talent can provide?

Day 4

1. Take a moment to review Absalom's plot to overthrow his father, King David. Was it God's will for Absalom to be king?

2. According to Absalom's story, what should our "I have to" *not* look like?

3. What does God promise Joshua?

4. Do you believe God will give you every place you set your foot? Why or why not?

Day 5

1. What does Ittai's "I have to" look like? Which of his characteristics of loyalty resonate with you most?

2. As you think back on this week, what "I have to" is God forming in your life? Do you feel fear, excitement, or both? Why?

Watch Session 2 at Christyfay.com: What Is "I Have To"?

MAKING SPACE
FOR "I HAVE TO"

Day 1: Fear's Fury
Exodus 2

One of my four-year-old's favorite things to do after arriving home from school or errands or wherever we've been is to dash inside and stand in one of several doorways I must walk through to make it to the kitchen/family room. "What's the password?" he will shout excitedly as his throws his arms and legs in an X-like pose across the opening. Usually the password isn't too difficult to figure out, and generally involves the name Mom or Dad or that of one of his three siblings. It's a very sweet ritual. Except when I'm in a hurry. Then it's not so cute.

All of us, at some point, have either found ourselves or will find ourselves at the threshold of some type of opportunity. It can feel like we are perched at the doorstep, standing on the brink, peeking inside, and longing to go in, and yet when we attempt to move forward, something blocks the way. Fear, anxiety, insecurity, mistrust, and a million other party poopers have flung their arms out, firm and stubborn, refusing to budge, determined to deter us from our adventure.

Now what?

This week, for us, is all about finding our password. Of course, if it were as easy as just one little word, we would all be living out our "I have to" unashamedly and unbridled. In reality, calling out the party poopers and telling them to get lost is extraordinarily difficult. I pray and hope that, together, we can find the courage to give them the what-for and kick them to the curb where they belong.

Let's move to the text that will guide us, Exodus chapter two. You will most likely recognize this story. It's an epic one, and for that reason it has been retold in all kinds of forms and forums through the years.

It begins with a woman, as most great stories do, giving birth to a son. Unfortunately, the world she has birthed him into is filled with hatred. This includes a maniacal leader who has begun to feel threatened by the increasingly large number of Israelites (God's people enslaved in Egypt) inhabiting his land. In an effort to achieve some form of population control, he mandates that all Israelite baby boys under the age of two be put to death. This is the context. Now read Exodus 2:1–10 and answer these questions.

What is Moses' nationality? (Exodus 2:1)

Who becomes Moses' adoptive mother? (Exodus 2:10)

We will pick up again at this spot in a moment. For now, hold the image of my son's arms stretched across the doorway, because Moses is standing at the precipice of an "I have to" that will alter his entire life. But, as there often is, something stands in his way. Let's find out what. Read Exodus 2:11–15.

There are a few words that are especially important to this text; take careful note of them. Fill in the blanks below and then circle those same words.

He [Moses] _____ an Egyptian beating a Hebrew, one of his own people (Exodus 2:11, NIV).

Looking this way and that and seeing no one, he _____ the Egyptian and hid him in the sand (Exodus 2:12).

There is something particularly interesting about these two words, "saw" and "killed"—many versions substitute the word *strike* for killed—being used in this context. Mostly because these two words are frequently used in conjunction with the work of God. Moses "sees" the oppression of Israel much like God is about to take notice or "see" the plight of His people (Exodus 2:25, 3:7–9, 4:31, 5:19). One Bible commentator writes: "Moses is no disinterested observer and, having seen (as God will see) Israel's oppression, takes the initiative to do what he can about it."[26]

Moses then kills, or "strikes," the Egyptian. The word for the verb *strike* in Hebrew is *nakah*, and it will later be used in association with God's striking of the Egyptians (12:12, 13, 29; 9:15; 7:16, 25). "The use of the same verb suggests that Moses' action was not considered inappropriate by the narrator, but it anticipates God's rather than Israel's activity."[27]

There is something about the connectivity of these two verbs (used in relation to both Moses' and God's work) that has deep meaning for you and me. Have you ever sensed a call or an "I have to" rising in your spirit? Ever felt so pulled toward something or someone that you cannot stop thinking about it, or them? Yes? Well, have you ever run after that "I have to" with such speed and tenacity that you find yourself well ahead of God in the whole thing?

This is what's happening to Moses. He sees his own—his *brethren*, is what the word indicates[28]—and his heart is moved with compassion. Now it's not this first part that goes all wrong. Being moved by compassion is never a bad thing, unless it leads to anger, the kind of anger that propels you to roll up your sleeves and take matters into your own hands. This isn't the kind of righteous anger the Bible talks about in relation to God. It may have begun that way for Moses, but it doesn't end that way. Moses' anger is compulsive and rooted in selfish ambition. It's the "I-can-fix-it-on-my-own" kind of anger, one void of anyone else's help and apart from God. It's the kind of anger that leaves an Egyptian dead and buried in the sand.

Boy, can I identify. I'm a go-getter. I'm a no-time-like-the-present kind of girl. I don't like waiting on God and trusting Him to do, in the future, what I can clearly do right now! Of course, the outcome is questionable, and there are frequently casualties. Now, how about you? Can you identify? Can you recall a time where you took matters into your own hands? What was the outcome? Describe it below.

If there wasn't enough proof in the text that Moses forges ahead outside of God's timing, there's even greater evidence in the interaction between Moses and two Hebrew

---

26 Terence E. Fretheim, *Exodus: Interpretation: A Bible Commentary for Teaching and Preaching* (Westminster John Knox Press), Kindle Edition, 42.

27 Ibid, 43.

28 James Strong, LLD, STD, *Strong's Expanded Exhaustive Concordance of the Bible* (Nashville: Thomas Nelson, 2010), 241.

slaves that takes place the next day. Moses is unable to wrap his head around the fact that, in the midst of Egyptian enslavement and torture, two men, on the same side of things no less, would be fighting, duking it out with each other. "Why are you hitting your fellow Hebrew?" Moses asks (Exodus 2:13). One looks up and asks him, "Who made you ruler and judge over us?" (Exodus 2:14).

It's a question Moses will have to deal with before he can chase His call. You see, the problem is that God hasn't made him ruler or judge *yet*. He will, but he hasn't yet. We must caution ourselves against chasing after our "I have to" before we have fully submitted ourselves to God's author-

ONE BIBLE COMMENTATOR WRITES: "MOSES IS NO DISINTERESTED OBSERVER AND, HAVING SEEN (AS GOD WILL SEE) ISRAEL'S OPPRESSION, TAKES THE INITIATIVE TO DO WHAT HE CAN ABOUT IT."

ity and sovereign schedule. We can't make ourselves rulers and leaders; only God can do that. And often, he has some work to do *in* us before He will choose to work through us.

The Hebrew poses one more question before these two men and Moses part ways. "Are you thinking of killing me as you killed the Egyptian?" This is Moses' caught-in-the-act moment. What he thought he had executed in secrecy has been observed by at least one other person, maybe more. How does Moses feel, and what does he say after this? Read Exodus 2:14–16.

What does Pharaoh do when he hears of this incident? What does Moses do in response?

Moses is afraid, and because he is afraid, he runs. This is a familiar story for me. Is it for you? Standing at the threshold, peeking in at your impending "I have to," and finding yourself flooded with all kinds of emotion. Does fear rise for you like it does for me, like it did for Moses? And is one of your responses to run?

In a moment, everything about Moses' life has changed. His cushy and comfortable home within the walls of the palace, his identity as an Egyptian, and any hope he might have had as the next in line for the throne—all of this comes crashing down around him. Of course, there also happens to be a very real threat on his physical life as well. Now, we will never know whether these events unfolded the way they did because Moses attempted in his own strength to do what God and only God could do. Or if Moses' discovery of his call would have caused this kind of disruption regardless. I have a feeling it might have been a bit smoother if he had trusted God to unravel his "I have to," only because I speak from experience on this particular front.

What I do know is our "I have to" may conjure up a fair amount of fear, and that might be the understatement of the century. Our most frequent tendency, like that of Moses, is to run. We recognize when we are feeling called or compelled to do something, and we also know just what kind of repercussions it might cause. We know we may have to say good-bye to our lives as we know them. And that, dear friends, can be a horrifying thought.

Has fear ever made you run? Are you about to strap on your running shoes right now? Why? Write about that time in the space below.

Let me close today with another convicting and insightful thought from comedian Jim Carrey.

"Now fear is going to be a player in your life. You get to decide how much. You can spend your whole life imagining ghosts worrying about the pathway to the future, but all there will ever be is what is happening here in the decisions we make in this moment[,] which are based in either love or fear. So many of us choose our path out of fear disguised as practicality."[29]

We must choose what could be the greatest adventure of our lives. Or will we choose the path of "fear disguised as practicality"? When it's put that way, it doesn't seem as difficult a choice to make.

---

29 Jim Carrey, Commencement Address, speech presented at Maharishi University of Management, Fairfield, IA, May 2014.

Day 2: Dreaming Backwards
Exodus 2:15–4:17

I read a beautiful short story in Marina Keegan's book *The Opposite of Loneliness* that I haven't been able to shake loose in my brain. It's stuck with me the same way a bowl of hearty oatmeal seems to stick, somewhere deep within. The story centers around the collision of two lives: Anna, a woman who finds herself past the middle of her life, still unsure of what she's doing on earth and convinced she suffers from every illness under the sun, with the exception of what is actually plaguing her; and Sam, a master's student at divinity school with a sort of occupational hazard. Sam is blind. Both are part of the Visually Impaired Assistant program through the local library. Sam is there for obvious reasons; Anna is there under a directive from her doctor, who insists that "purpose and routine" are what she needs more than any medication.

One interaction the two share is especially fascinating for our purposes.

"I miss dreaming forwards," Anna said.
"What?"
"I dream backwards now. You won't believe how backwards you'll dream some-day . . . "
"I didn't think dreams had directions." [Sam's] broken eyes managed a smile . . .
"I dream of the past, of things that could have happened, or should have happened or never happened. You dream of your future . . . . "[30]

Dreaming backwards. Never in a million years would I have arrived at that concept on my own, but when I read it, I realized it's the most perfectly poetic way to describe what we do. Kind of like that mega high school football star whose career-ending injury leaves him on the sidelines of life. Unable to land or keep a real job, locked up in his dingy living room eating Spaghetti-O's out of can, watching old highlight reels. Or the mother of three who can't get out of bed in the morning, spending her days looking at pictures of a previous life while her kids are at school. The life she lived before her ex dumped her for a newer, younger, bustier version.

I see myself in these characters I've just written about, not because either of those stories are exactly mine. More so, because I too am prone to "dreaming backwards." Sometimes it's easier to reminisce about times gone by rather than face the present and our often-underwhelming current circumstances. But I think it's high time we drove a "Wrong Direction" sign deep into the territory of our dreams (the backwards ones, I mean.)

---

30 Marina Keegan, *The Opposite of Loneliness* (New York: Scribner, Simon and Schuster, Inc., 2014), 56–57.

Let's stick with our text and the story of Moses. We only scratched the surface of his incredible story yesterday. Our focus will center around Exodus chapters three and four. In order to bridge yesterday and today, first read Exodus 2:15–3:10.

Who appears to Moses in the flames of fire? (Exodus 3:2)

What does He tell Moses to do? (Exodus 3:10)

Yesterday we talked about how Moses rushes forward with his "I have to" before God grants him authority to do so. In today's account, we see God decisively handing out Moses' "I have to."

"So now, go. I am sending you to Pharaoh to bring my people the Israelites out of Egypt" (Exodus 2:10, NIV).

Clear. As. Day.

This is Moses' "Arise and go" moment, and much like Jonah's, it involves forward motion toward a Nineveh of sorts. Of course, we will see that, just as we learned for Jonah, Moses is more comfortable dreaming backwards than forwards.

Now let's track Moses' response to God's call. Read Exodus 3:11–4:17. As you do, complete these instances of Moses' five separate objections.

1. *But Moses said to God, "Who am _____ that _____ should go to Pharaoh and _____ the Israelites out of Egypt?"* (Exodus 3:11).

2. *Moses said to God, "Suppose I go to the Israelites and say to them, 'The God of your fathers has _____ me to you,' and they ask me, 'What is his name?' Then what shall I _____ them?"* (Exodus 3:13).

3. *Moses answered, "What if they do not _____ me or _____ to me and say, 'The Lord did not appear to you'"?* (Exodus 4:4).

4. *Moses said to the Lord, "Pardon your servant, Lord. I have never been _____, neither in the past nor since you have spoken to your servant. I am slow of speech and tongue"* (Exodus 4:10).

5. *But Moses said, "Pardon your servant, Lord. Please _____ someone else"* (Exodus 4:13).

These are some major excuses. When I first read through this litany of objections, I thought: Jeez, Moses, come on. Get it together. Can't you man up and just do it already?

How easy it is to look at the plank in someone else's eye while your own is filled with its share of junk. I have done this! I too am filled with excuses. I've said things like this to myself, God, or others.

"Well, God, why would you choose me? I'm dysfunctional, and there are clearly so many others you could choose for this task."

"When they ask me why in the world I am doing this? What kind of answer do I give? 'God told me to?' Who is going to buy that?"

"I'm not even convinced I can actually write (or sing, or manage other people, or whatever; you fill in the blank)."

"I'm pretty sure I shouldn't do this at all. I'm really not cut out for it."

Tell me these sound familiar to you as well! OK. Now I am going to ask you to be really honest. What is your "go to" or default excuse? We all have one. What's yours? Journal it here.

Before we go any further on the topic of Moses and his collection of objections, let's examine God's role in all this. What are His replies to Moses? Go ahead and make a list of God's various responses and the numerous ways He promises to aid Moses. I completed the first one to get us rolling.

1. Exodus 3:12 — "I will be with you."

2. Exodus 3:14 —

3. Exodus 3:18 —

4. Exodus 3:20 —

5. Exodus 3:21 —

6. Exodus 4:11 —

7. Exodus 4:14 —

For every excuse Moses drops, God has a compelling and persuasive counterpoint. Perhaps what is even more stunning about this interaction is that . . . there is an interaction at all! Moses is a human. And God is, well . . . God is God. You'd think the Holy One wouldn't be all that interested in dialoguing with His earthly subjects. It's certainly not absurd to think that the extraordinary wouldn't really want to mix with the ordinary. But this couldn't be further from the truth. As one commentator wrote, "The divine holiness is of such a character that it invites rather than repels human response, inviting Moses into genuine conversation. God does not demand a self-effacing Moses, but draws him out and works with him[,] warts and all."[31]

The fact that God would choose to use Moses for this incredible and weighty task is equally baffling and beautiful. But then He takes it a step further by not just choosing Moses but convincing him he is good enough and more than up to the task. This makes me breathe a deep and long sigh of relief. What is your response to this comforting truth?

31 Terence E. Fretheim, *Exodus: Interpretation: A Bible Commentary for Teaching and Preaching* (Westminster John Knox Press), 52. Kindle Edition.

Although I can completely identify with Moses and his many and varied excuses, there is one question the text compels me to ask. Why would Moses' first response be, "Why me?" Why not: "Why *not* me?" Of course, I recognize it's a distinctly human quality to doubt, especially our own abilities and capacities. It is normal, quite natural, to allow "Why me?" to be the dominant voice in our heads. But I think there is something else going with Moses beyond simple human predisposition.

Moses has walked this path before. He's played the hero. He's rallied around this cry to save the Israelites once already. It did not turn out so well. It left an Egyptian buried in the sand. It led him away from his adoptive family and into the desert. And so now, staring into the fire of a burning bush, Moses hears the voice of God call him back to the place he's spent the last forty years trying to forget.

It's no surprise he doesn't want to go.

Have you ever tried to do something that felt significant and important, but just didn't work out? In which you had your hopes dashed, your ego bruised, your dreams shattered? If you can recall feeling like this, record your thoughts in this space.

I wholeheartedly believe Moses was hurt badly that day back in Egypt. I'm quite sure, although the text doesn't tell us directly, he had been turning over the idea in his mind that he might be the one. Perhaps the only one sitting on the side of the Egyptians with enough power and pull to inaugurate true and lasting change for his fellow countrymen.

DREAMING BACKWARDS. NEVER IN A MILLION YEARS WOULD I HAVE ARRIVED AT THAT CONCEPT ON MY OWN, BUT WHEN I READ IT, I REALIZED IT'S THE MOST PERFECTLY POETIC WAY TO DESCRIBE WHAT WE DO.

Maybe you've tried and tried for a child, and months have passed, then years, and all you're left with is a whole bunch of negative pregnancy tests and a broken heart. Maybe you've quit your job before, tried something new, gone back to school, only to meet the same feeling of disappointment again and again. You've given up hope searching for that one thing you and only you were made to do.

Maybe you're sensing God calling you back. Back to the land you ran from, a land filled with heartache, missed opportunities, deserted dreams.

Moses can relate. And so can I. Somehow, at the end all those excuses, Moses says yes to God. It's not pretty, and he sure does put up a compelling fight, but in the end God's vision for Moses' life triumphs. This interaction between God and his chosen one is proof that we can converse and even argue with God. We can lay it all out before Him. He'll listen, He'll intervene, and He'll go as far as to alter His plans to accommodate us. (I doubt that including Moses' brother Aaron as spokesman to Pharaoh was actually part of God's plan A!) If we're brave enough to say yes, we will be thrust into the center of an epic story. A story in which we watch miracles unfold before our very eyes. A story rich with redemption, one embedded with the kind of grace that transforms everything it touches.

So, today, what will you choose? Will you dream backwards or forwards?

Day 3: The Great Reversal
Genesis 25:19–26

I couldn't find my cell phone the other day. This isn't an unusual occurrence. In the midst of chasing around after four kids I tend to put it down in strange places. I get pulled one direction to help with homework and then yanked the other way to wipe a nose or fix hair or whatever, and I forget about the weird place I laid it down. Later, when I go back to the email I was trying to write or the phone call I was about to make, I can't find my phone anywhere. And the search begins. And let's be honest, there is nothing more frustrating, nothing that makes you want to tear your hair out more, than not being able to find the one thing you need when you need it. At this point my frustration generally leaks out and lands all over my kids.

"What did you do with it?"

"I know you were playing Ninja Run on it, so where did you leave it?"

More frequently than I'd like to admit, my oldest son, who rarely misses a beat, looks at me with an air of elitism and says, "Mom, your phone is in your back pocket." Or, "Mom, it's tucked in your sports bra." Yes, that's where I keep it sometimes when I'm wearing yoga pants, which basically means that is where I keep it 98 percent of the time!

"You're right," I begrudgingly acknowledge. There's nothing more humbling than realizing your eight-year-old is more astute than you are.

You then have to come to terms with the fact you just wasted the last twenty minutes of your life looking for something that was (literally) right under your nose.

Have you ever had this kind of experience? Use this question as a sort of icebreaker for our lesson today, and one that will span not only today's content but tomorrow's as well. Journal your experience here.

This is Jacob's story. There are few characters in the book of Genesis whom we meet at birth. Most we become acquainted with them midstory, sometimes even midconversation, which I suppose is the way it was intended. There's something endearing about a God who invites us *into* a story. In His mind we've been a part of it from day one, whether we realize it or not.

Read about Jacob's entrance into the world in Genesis 25:19–24.

Now reread Genesis 25:23. In a sense, this is the end of the story for Jacob, even before his story has begun. It's his phone-in-the-back-pocket and glasses-on-the-head-the-whole-time-you've-been-searching moment. I'm going to spend the rest of the next two days of study showing us why. For now, and for the sake of emphasis, fill in the holes in the following Scriptures.

The Lord said to her, "Two nations are in your womb, and two peoples from within you will be separated; one people will be stronger than the other, and the _____ will serve the _____" (Genesis 35:23, NIV).

There are two critical points that surface from this short text. The first is that Jacob enters into an existence that is wrought with conflict: "Two people from within you will be separated; one people will be stronger than the other." This is substantiated by the way in which Esau and Jacob physically enter the world. Genesis 25:26 paints a picture of Jacob's appearance. Describe it here.

From the beginning, Jacob is pictured as one striving for something that is ultimately just beyond reach. He's grasping at the heel of his brother, and although this is a physical description of what happens, it's also a foreshadowing of what is to come. For this reason, Jacob spends a large portion of his life chasing after his brother's position as firstborn—and the benefits that accompany it. Of course, we can clearly see Jacob is striving to attain a favor that has already been granted to him: "And the older will serve the younger."

One commentator, in an effort to describe this very real battle Jacob enters into from birth, writes, "From the beginning, Jacob is destined to be a man of combat. The paradoxical marks of gift and conflict dominate the Jacob narrative."[32] The two, gift and conflict, continue to dominate the storyline of our lives even today. Here's a question I'd like you to ponder. Have you ever had difficulty accepting a gift? Perhaps it came from a close friend or a spouse or maybe even a stranger. It could have been monetary or more abstract in nature, like the gift of another's time. What was the gift, and why was it difficult to receive?

---

32 Walter Brueggemann, *Genesis: Interpretation: A Bible Commentary for Teaching and Preaching* (Presbyterian Publishing Corporation). Kindle Edition.

I am no mind reader, but I think it's a fair assumption that the majority of your answers had something to do with not feeling worthy or good enough to receive the gift. Most of us have a hard time accepting things for free because we feel we should have done something to earn or deserve them. Our American economy is built on capitalism: the freedom of the individual to buy and sell outside governmental control. This only works when there is a give and take. A seller and a buyer. A marketer and a consumer. Within the context of this system, if something is free, it's immediately suspicious. Which is why the concept of *grace* is so difficult for the human mind to comprehend. A God who would give without demanding anything in return—*this can't be possible*, we think. And so we often find ourselves like Jacob, chasing after something that was gifted to us from the very beginning. Sometimes because we don't think we are worthy of it, and sometimes because we didn't even know the gift was there in the first place.

FROM THE BEGINNING, JACOB IS PICTURED AS ONE STRIVING FOR SOMETHING THAT IS ULTIMATELY JUST BEYOND REACH. HE'S GRASPING AT THE HEEL OF HIS BROTHER.

Which leads to a second point we can pull from our text. When God speaks to Rebekah, he reveals something, not only about her two sons, but about his character as well. God was not, is not, nor ever will be hemmed in by any human presumption or intention. He doesn't play by our rules, not just because He doesn't have to, or because He doesn't want to. Often, it's for the sake of our own good that He chooses to ignore our petty and inconsequential rules and our frivolously placed boundaries. In one sense, Esau *should* be first; he was born first and therefore should be rewarded as such. But God chooses Jacob, and that's the end of that.

God has the power to make promises and keep them in spite of any human expectations. This is the premise of the Exodus narrative: God makes a distinction for Israel against Egypt (Exodus 11:7). That is the premise of the ministry of Jesus: the poor, the mourning, the meek, the hungry, and the merciful are the heirs to the kingdom (see Matthew 5:3–7). This God does not align himself only with the obviously valued ones, with only the firstborn.[33]

Many scholars draw a line of connection between Genesis 25:23— "and the older will serve the younger"—and Jesus' words in Matthew 20:16: "So the last shall be first, and the first shall be last." It's easy to see why.[34] Long before Jesus ever wore sandals and walked the earth, God was out to prove things are not always as they seem, especially under His reign and rule. About this, theologian Walter Brueggemann writes, "Jacob is announced as a visible expression of God's remarkable graciousness in the face of conventional definitions of reality and prosperity. Jacob is a scandal from the beginning. The powerful grace of God is a scandal. It upsets the way we would organize life."[35]

I wonder how differently Jacob's life would have played out if he only understood the true character of God's grace. Perhaps he would have spent less time chasing after his brother's birthright and blessing (the topic of tomorrow's lesson) and more time trusting that the God who promised "the older will serve the younger" would stay true to His word.

We read this story in light of the life and death of Jesus. We understand even more clearly, far more than Jacob did, that we serve a God of inversions, where washing the feet of others defines real leadership and where death on a cross produces true life. Nothing has to be as we think it has to be. The story of Jacob "affirms that we are not fated to the way the world is presently organized."[36] Can I get an amen? Do you see what this means? Whether we think we are qualified or unqualified for our "I have to," it really doesn't matter. All we need to know is God has given us something to do, an opportunity to be a gift to the world around us. Whether it fits with our plan, or our friends' plans, or our parents' plans, or whomever-else-on-God's-green-earth's plan, it is *His* plan. And that is enough!

Have you ever questioned God's call on your life because it didn't align with someone else's definition of what you should or shouldn't be doing? Are you walking through something like that now? Write about that below.

33 Ibid.

34 Ibid.

35 Ibid.

36 Ibid.

What is your reaction to the statement that "the powerful grace of God is a scandal. It upsets the way we would organize life"?

- human nature to think we don't get anything unless its earned...

Day 4: Wearing Someone Else's Clothes
Genesis 25:27–34; Genesis 27

I began yesterday by writing about losing my cell phone, searching for it for way too long, then finding it tucked in my back pocket or sports bra! I asserted that Jacob's life becomes a living and breathing example of what it looks like to strive and search for something that's actually there the whole time. Today's text will serve as further proof.

Let's get started, reading Genesis 25:27–34.

As it is with most families, our firstborn, Oliver, and our secondborn, Wesley, could not be more different. They are both boys and were born only eighteen months apart, so in theory you wouldn't think there would be that many dissimilarities. Oh, but there are. In looks, to a certain extent, but even more so in personality. My husband and I love to highlight their distinct and pronounced differences through one simple story. At a cousin's birthday party each was served a large piece of cake. Oliver examined it scrupulously, calculating a plan to eat his serving with the greatest level of equal parts enjoyment and orderliness. He even asked, "How should I eat this, Dad?" While Oliver pondered, Wesley put his face directly into the cake and began eating it doggie-style: no hands or forks and no regrets! Enough said.

Much like my oldest boys, the brothers of this Genesis account, although twins, have very little in common. In the columns below, write what we know about both their looks and personalities.

Jacob   **Esau**

You now have a completed visual of the many and varied ways in which Jacob and Esau differ. It's probably best to also include a record of which parent favors which child. It's important to note this since it's Rebekah's favoritism of Jacob that drives much of the storyline. Before we go any further, we should ask an important question: What's the big deal with the birthright? Look up the following passages and fill in the blanks with what we learn about a family's birthright.

Deuteronomy 21:17 (NIV): *The firstborn receives a* ___two___ ___share___ *of the inheritance.*

1 Chronicles 5:1, 2: *The sons of Reuben the firstborn of Israel . . . (he was the firstborn, but when he defiled his father's marriage bed, his rights as firstborn were given to the sons of Joseph son of Israel; so he could not be listed in the genealogical record in accordance with his birthright, and though Judah was the* ___strongest___ *of his brothers and a* ___ruler___ *came from him, the rights of the firstborn belonged to Joseph).*

"Passages like Deuteronomy 21:17 and 1 Chronicles 5:1–2 tell us the *birthright* involved both a material and a spiritual dynamic. The son of the birthright received a double portion of the inheritance, and he also became the head of the family and the spiritual leader upon the passing of the father."[37] In this particular family, the firstborn was the one to inherit the promise given to the grandfather of the brothers, Abraham (Genesis 12).

In other words, the birthright is a big deal! The fact that Jacob, the much keener of the two, is willing to capitalize on his brother's weakness certainly proves a point concerning his character. On the other hand, the fact that Esau is willing to trade his rights as firstborn for a bowl of soup just because his stomach is grumbling certainly gives us insight into *his* character.

The scenario painted at the tail end of Genesis 25 is only half the story. Turn to Genesis 27 and you will find the other half. This is one of the rare times I'll ask you to read a bit more, but it's an incredibly significant moment in lives of both Jacob and Esau, and worth diving deeper. So please read the entirety of Genesis 27.

Let's begin, as we did above, with a definition of the concept of blessing. It's not an easy thing to wrap our heads around because there isn't a counterpart in today's culture that carries the same weight and gravity as a blessing did in the days of Isaac, Jacob, and Esau. I can't say it any better than Walter Brueggemann. In his commentary on Genesis, Brueggemann breaks the definition of blessing into several key components:

1. **The blessing is intergenerational in nature**: "The pursuit of blessing characterizes existence as intergenerational. Parents and children have a deep stake in each others' destinies."

2. **The blessing is a symbolic action**: "The narrative presumes that symbolic actions have genuine and abiding power. Symbolic actions (like laying on hands) are not empty gestures signifying nothing. This ritual act is a decisive event in which something has been done irrevocably."

3. **The blessing is a spoken word with great meaning and power**: "This narrative assumes and affirms that spoken words shape human life."

---

37 David Guzik, *Verse by Verse Commentary: Genesis* (Santa Barbara, California: Enduring Word Media, 2012).

4. **The blessing shapes the future**: This narrative "understands that power, the capacity to shape the future, lies not in weapons and arms, but in the use of language, gesture, and symbol."[38]

When Isaac gifts the blessing to Jacob, it is irreversible, powerful, significant, symbolic, and sacred. It has deep and profound ramifications and alters the destinies of both sons. Of course, even the power of the blessing cannot surpass God's power. We will discuss how Jacob eventually discovers his true identity in the blessing that comes from his God. For now, the text has a great deal to teach us.

What I find most fascinating about this story is the lengths that both Rebekah and Jacob are willing to go to secure the blessing. It's a complicated plan filled with all kinds of trickery. Reread Genesis 27:15, 16 and fill in the blanks.

Then Rebekah took the best _____ of Esau her older son, which she had in the house, and put them on her younger son. She also _____ his hands and the smooth part of his neck with the goatskins (Genesis 27:15, 16).

Jacob finds himself dressed in the smelly clothes of his hunter-brother, goatskins fastened to his hands and neck, standing before his father. You might think his costume and hairy mask would be enough for at least a momentary pause of self-evaluation. Maybe even long enough for him to entertain a few thoughts. Perhaps something like:

"What am I doing?"

"Isn't it kind of ridiculous that I have to wear my brother's clothes to secure this blessing?"

"Perhaps my mom and I have taken it one step too far this time."

However, goatskin-covered arms and stinky clothes are far from enough to stop Jacob from executing his plan. In fact, he will go on to lie, not just once or twice, but three separate times to his father. Oh, and not white lies told behind Isaac's back, but blatant and pronounced lies to his dying father's face. Let's play a game of detective and work together to uncover the lies. I found the first one; you find the other two.

Lie 1 "I am Esau your firstborn." (Genesis 27:19)

Lie 2 _____ (Genesis 27:20)

Lie 3 _____ (Genesis 27:22)

Quick story: I once received a green sweatshirt from my step-cousin. It was a hand-me-down, so I inherited it with a few loose strings and worn-down spots on the material. But when I was done with it, I'm pretty sure any and all life had been sucked dry from that poor little sweatshirt. I wore it. And when I say I wore it, I mean I wore it *all the*

---

38 Brueggemann, *Genesis: Interpretation: A Bible Commentary for Teaching and Preaching.* Kindle Edition.

time. I'm five years younger than my step-cousin, which meant that anything she did was inherently cool. She had curly hair, so I wanted curly hair. She cut it short, and then I wanted to cut my hair short. She got her nose pierced, and when I was old enough, I got mine pierced too. Thinking back, there was really nothing special about that green sweatshirt. In fact, it was actually kind of ugly. But when I put it on I fancied myself as cool as my big cousin, and for that reason the sweatshirt was the greatest article of clothing I owned.

My point here is all of us can be a little bit like Jacob. We can put on other people's clothes, metaphorically speaking, at times. We aren't comfortable with ourselves, perhaps because we were never told we were smart enough, good enough, attractive enough, successful enough, fill-in-the-blank enough. Or perhaps because, even though we were told all those things, we couldn't or didn't want to believe they were true. After a while it became easier to just pretend to be someone else. To hide behind a mask of apathy, anger, or self-loathing. To wear the skins of sufficiency, adequacy, or even of happiness and success. Sometimes to blend in and sometimes to live a life we think we deserve but won't actually work to obtain.

> MY POINT HERE IS ALL OF US CAN BE A LITTLE BIT LIKE JACOB. WE CAN PUT ON OTHER PEOPLE'S CLOTHES, METAPHORICALLY SPEAKING, AT TIMES. WE AREN'T COMFORTABLE WITH OURSELVES.

"It's OK if I have to lie to keep it up." "I'm just looking out for me." "Just trying to do my best to get by in this dog-eat-dog world." These are the kinds of lies we tell ourselves, churn around within, and spit back out. I have to make my own destiny, and even if I have to sacrifice myself and pretend to be someone I'm not, it's worth it if it secures in me a place of honor, esteem, and high regard.

"I'll do what I have to do to get my blessing." This is the line Jacob fed himself, and it's the same line we too often feed ourselves.

This topic of discussion is far from easy. I realize I'm treading on thin ice in many ways. No one wants to admit that the persona they display is actually a facade. But if we are going to step into our "I have to's," we must make space. And making space looks like stripping down out of that other person's clothes and casting aside the goatskins. Then and only then can we begin to feel at home in our own skin and dress ourselves in our own clothes.

We will spend a lot of time tomorrow reflecting more on this topic. For now, let's close with one question:

Have you ever put on someone else's clothes (I'm speaking figuratively)? What kinds of lies did you tell yourself and others along the way?

· We hold onto things God has connected us of

· if we are to take hold of something, we often have to let go of something else...

phil 3:11-14

- we have to sometimes let go of other storylines that are trying to dominate our life.
Takee hold of the story God has for you life vs. other people expect of you or you expect of your self

Day 5: Gains and Losses
Philippians 3:1–12

We spent time yesterday talking about clothes and goatskins. I asked some tough questions, ones that didn't come with easy answers. But I do hope, dear friends, that you found the courage that comes from God to wade through the waters of adversity. I will warn you: today I'm going to ask you to wade in a bit deeper. The water might feel cold on your midsection; it might shock you a bit. But after a while, you'll realize the water isn't all that cold, your body will adjust, and you will find that all the adversity was preparing you for an even greater adventure. You're about to ride the wave that is your "I have to," and it will be both exhilarating and terrifying, and in the best way possible! You are about to discover you are capable of things you never thought possible, and that your dreams, much like objects in your rearview mirror, are much closer than they appear.

Yesterday we talked about dressing ourselves in someone else's clothes. Today we're going to talk about the many ways we let others dress us, often without our knowing it. There are people and experiences that have influenced us beyond measure—positively, negatively, or equal parts both.

When our children are infants we're responsible for dressing them. Mostly because they can't hold their heads up or sit up independently, never mind shimmying a T-shirt over their heads (which, by the way, are often too large for the smallish opening designated for their noggins). So we choose their outfits. But almost all parents remember the day when they look us in the eye and say, "No. I don't want to wear that." We say goodbye to our nicely coordinated ensembles and hello to clashing colors and mismatched plaids. But this is an important stage of development, right? At least, this is what we tell ourselves. Our kids are asserting their independence and forming their own opinions. And our role as parents is to affirm that, even if means they wear red cowboy boots and Batman capes to school.

What is interesting is that, although we are quick to encourage individuality with our toddler-sized children, we are not so quick to do the same with our teenaged children when they decide to take a gap year and "find themselves." (Which, conveniently, will take place in Bali.) And, of course, if we are to reflect back on our own journey, we find that our parents or grandparents had just as much difficulty relinquishing control. The truth is—and it's a little harsh—sometimes we are still letting other people (our friends, our spouse, our parents, to name a few) dress us. It's time to dress ourselves. Even if it's a bit awkward and our buttons end up in the wrong holes.

Skye Jethani, in his book *Futureville*, wrote: "Whoever shapes our vision of tomorrow wields enormous influence over our lives. The choices we make, the values that guide us, the word we pursue, and the people we become are all shaped by the way we think about the future. Sometimes those influences are positive, offering us a sense of purpose and hope, but they can also be damaging and cause us to be shortsighted and selfish."[39]

Let's take a moment to examine some of these influences. To do that I want to guide us to a text written by the apostle Paul. This time it comes from his letter to the church at Philippi. A small bit of background: there are certain Jewish members of the community at Philippi who are forcing some of the Gentile Christians within their group to undergo circumcision. Circumcision for the Jews is a right of ancestry or heritage, a marking that not only delineated them from other cultures and people-groups but marked them as God's chosen.[40] In the beginning of Philippians chapter three, Paul asserts that circumcision of the Gentile members is not only unnecessary, it is actually a way of placing confidence in the flesh. "The main thing Paul meant by the flesh here (and often in Galatians and Romans) is the pride of physical descent cherished by the Jews,"[41] writes theologian N. T. Wright.

Now that you have the context, take a moment and read Philippians 3:1–12. As you go, make a list of all the reasons Paul could have used to place confidence in the flesh.

1. Circumcised on the eighth day.

2.

3.

4.

5.

6.

7.

Paul was as Jewish as anyone can get. He was born into the right family, with the appropriate lineage and heritage, and he followed the law without fault—and yet none of that mattered in light of his "I have to." To use the language from our introduction for this week, Paul "should" have been a Jewish Pharisee. But instead, from the moment he met Jesus on the road to Damascus (Acts 9:1–19), he surrendered himself to his "must," a vagabond in chains for the cause of Christ.

---

39 Skye Jethani, *Futureville* (Nashville: Nelson Books, 2013).

40 N. T. Wright, *Philippians: 18 Studies for Individuals and Groups* (Downers Grove, IL: Intervarsity Press, 2009), 38.

41 Ibid.

Now that you've read Paul's list, I would like you to make your own. What reasons do you have to put confidence in the flesh? What is it you feel you "should" be doing?

Before you do, allow the following paragraphs to serve as your warning.

What you may come to discover is that you aren't necessarily meant to be the real estate entrepreneur like your father or the stay-at-home mom like your mother. You might discover your law degree, however valuable to your pocketbook, has very little to do with the heartbeat of your "I have to." It is quite possible you will discover you are not meant to walk the same path as the rock star you idolize, or the author whose words touched your soul, or the athlete your eight-year-old mind once dreamed you would become.

And the truth is, that's OK.

It's exceptionally difficult to scratch away the surface of those once closely held hopes and aspirations to find there's not a true calling underneath. You may very well have to come face-to-face with the fact that you will disappoint people, some of whom are your closest family members and friends. And while, hopefully, this disappointment quickly diminishes in the shadow of your "I have to," the reality is that it may not.

So now it's your time to reflect. There is nothing special about the number seven provided below. Feel free to write more, or less, than seven in this space.

1.

2.

3.

4.

5.

6.

7.

Now let's reread Philippians 3:7 and fill in the blanks.

But whatever were _____ to me I now consider _____ for the sake of Christ.

Let's start with the fact that at one point Paul's list, his reasons to put confidence in the flesh, were considered gains to him. Some of those reasons existed purely because of birth. He was born a Jew. Some of the reasons came about because of the choices his family made for him, such as "circumcised on the eighth day." And some of those reasons he worked diligently for: "as for righteousness based on the law, faultless." It was no effortless task to remain faithful to all the laws set forth in the Hebrew Torah.

Perhaps you can identify. Maybe birth alone qualified you for some kind of significant and valuable inheritance. Maybe your dad worked two jobs to send you to school to get your masters degree in architecture. Or perhaps you worked tirelessly to earn that position in your law firm, and now it all seems for nothing. Maybe your "gains" were big ones, just like Paul's.

I think that's why his story is so compelling. He lost it all. His standing. The respect of his peers. And we aren't told this, but I think it's a very real possibility his family disowned him. For Paul, however, this matters little. "What is more, I consider everything a loss because of the surpassing worth of knowing Christ Jesus my Lord, for whose sake I have lost all things. I consider them garbage that I may gain Christ" (Philippians 3:8).

Now, I know that not all of us can look at our list of gains and speak over them, like Paul, "I consider these all a loss for the sake of Christ."

So start with one thing from your list and read it out loud. Think about holding it in your hand, and instead of grasping it will all your might, imagine your hand releasing the tension and opening.

Now, say out loud—yes, I really want you to do this, to say it aloud: "Whatever were gains to me I now consider loss for the sake of Christ."

You might only be able to whisper it. But I believe that, over time, you will be able to scream it at the top of your lungs, and actually mean it.

Today, start with one.

Tomorrow, if you're ready, move on to another.

Let go of your "should" to embrace your "must." Relinquish your "I want to's" to take hold of your "I have to."

You will not regret it.

"*. . . press on to take hold of that for which Christ took hold of me.*"

Every step of the way His promise is that He has you in His hands. Trust that.

WHEN ALL SIGNS POINT TO "I HAVE TO"

The Setup

I have a terrible internal compass. What I mean by that is I can barely figure out right from left, never mind north from south and east from west. I am that person who, when asked which way to turn, has to (stealthily) glance down at my hands and pretend I'm holding a pen to be reminded which hand is which. Then, and only then, can I confidently pronounce, "It's a left at such and such street." It's a little embarrassing.

To combat my poor sense of direction, I've learned to identify certain landmarks to determine my location. For example, I can't tell you the name of my best friend's street, but what I can tell you is there is a fire hydrant directly before you have to turn right. If I can even in fact decipher in that moment which way is right!

I frequently get lost at the Phoenix airport. I can get around inside with few issues, but picking up and dropping people off is my nightmare. It's a lot like the Bermuda Triangle for me. I can get in, but I can't get out. My husband always says, "Just follow the signs. All you need to do is look for the sign marked I-10 West, and you are set." For me, that's far easier said than done. I have found myself halfway to Tucson more than a few times before I can trace my initial blunder back to that sharp right turn I missed attempting to exit the airport.

This is why we need signs. And if you're me, not just one or two, but about ten, strategically placed along the route to ensure safe arrival at the end destination.

55

Can you identify?

It's this way with life too, isn't it? We need a lot of signposts if we are ever going to get where we want to go.

I took my four-year-old to a friend's house the other day. We had never been there before, so everything was unfamiliar and therefore a bit intimidating for him. He had to go to the bathroom; what else is new? He bounded out in front of me headed to the facilities, but he only took a few steps before he paused, glanced over his shoulder, and asked, "This way?"

"Yes." I pointed straight ahead.

His little feet took a few more steps and then, again: "This way, right?"

"Yep," I said, while thinking, *Buddy, it's only been a few more feet. Did you really think anything had changed?*

Of course, I do that too.

"This way, right, Lord?"

"You did say I should quit this job and apply for another one, yes?"

"I know we just had this conversation about ten minutes ago, but could you just give me one more sign that this is the man I'm supposed to marry?"

When it comes to big and often daunting decisions, we often need not just one or two signs, we need ten, eleven . . . or fifty.

If only signs from God were as simple and straightforward as road signs. "Caution": That relationship my cause more harm than good. "Watch for Children": You are about to get pregnant. "Exit 183 [in] 1/4 mile": There's a new path to be traveled, and it begins here.

It's not always easy to decipher the voice of God in our lives. We don't always understand our next steps with crystal clarity. So how can we know what we are supposed to do and where we are supposed to go? We desperately want to walk the right path, but what's the right path?

This week, I want to examine some stories from the Scriptures that will give us insight. Of course, there is no one road map that will work for everyone. There are no hard and fast formulas. If there were, that would mean we are all robots under the control of a God operating by manipulation and not love.

The cliché-riddled statement is true: "hindsight is always twenty-twenty." We may not always see our future with perfect focus. But we will be able to look back and clearly see the hand of God at work in our lives. And we can be absolutely sure of one thing: Wherever God will lead us, it will be good.

*The revelation of God is whole and pulls our lives together. The **signposts** of God are clear and point out the right road. The life-maps of God are right, showing the way to joy. The directions of God are plain and easy on the eyes. God's reputation is twenty-four-carat gold, with a lifetime guarantee. The decisions of God are accurate down to the nth degree"* (Psalm 19:7–9, MSG, emphasis added).

I want a life pulled together by God, moving along the right road and headed toward joy. So let's spend the next week trying to figure out how to do that.

Let's review these questions from week two of our personal study.

Day 1

1. In what way is the work of God connected to the work of Moses? In what ways does Moses rush ahead of God?

2. Have you ever gotten out ahead of God? Have you ever found yourself taking matters into your own hands? When, and how so?

3. What role has fear played in your life? Has it ever made you strap on your sneakers and start running? Elaborate.

Day 2

1. What's your response to the concept of dreaming backward? Have you ever found yourself spending more time reminiscing about your past then inhabiting your present and dreaming about your future?

2. Moses had a few excuses when it came to his "I have to." Do you have any? Is there one in particular you use more than others?

3. Can you identify with Moses in this story? Have you ever tried to do something, something that felt significant and important, and it just didn't work out? How do you see this deterring your moving forward with your "I have to"?

Day 3

1. How does Jacob make his appearance in the world? (Genesis 25:26)

2. Have you ever had a hard time accepting a gift from someone, monetary or otherwise? Can you recall a specific instance?

3. Have you ever questioned God's call on your life because it didn't align with someone else's definition of what you should or shouldn't be doing? Are you walking through something like that now? Write more about that in this space.

Day 4

1. Review your list from the second week under this day. How do Jacob and Esau differ?

2. What is the significance of the blessing?

3. How many lies does Jacob tell? What are they?

4. Have you ever put on someone else's clothes (I'm speaking figuratively)? What kinds of lies did you have to tell yourself and others along the way?

Day 5

1. What is it you feel you "should" be doing? Reference your list from day five, week two.

2. As a group, read Philippians 3:8 aloud. What might God be calling you to consider loss for the sake of Christ?

Watch Session 3 at Christyfay.com: Making Space for "I Have To"

its uncomfortable to let go of relationship or situations but thats when we grow

WHEN ALL SIGNS POINT TO "I HAVE TO"

Day 1: General Calling
Acts 10:1–8

As we dive into this week, I want to acknowledge that while we have two weeks of this study under our belts, and while some of you are 100 percent certain you have discovered your unique and personal "I have to," others are still searching. Do not allow insecurity to creep in, and do your very best, God helping you, to avoid the temptation of comparing yourself to those around you. We are all on our own journey with our own sets of calling and our own signposts. Be wary of striving to mold yourself into any image other than the one handcrafted for you by your Creator.

My prayer is that today's topic will challenge all of us wherever we find ourselves in this moment. But my deep desire is that our text will provide hope and encouragement, especially for those of you waiting on God for an "I have to" revelation.

Let's start again in the book of Acts. Today's passage has only eight verses, so go ahead and read Acts 10:1–8.

The main character in this passage is a man named Cornelius. Let's work together to assemble a list of his character traits; these are provided in the first three verses.

1. A _____ in the Italian Regiment.

2. He and his family were _____.

3. He was _____-fearing.

4. He gave _____ to those in need.

5. He prayed to God _____.

In today's culture, a title like Lt. (lieutenant) or Sgt. (sergeant) is indicative of much more than just a ranking in the armed forces; it's a glimpse into a person's character. Ironically, I am writing this on Veteran's Day. Today, social media has been flooded with words like *honor, respect, dignity, self-sacrifice,* and *courage,* and deservedly so, as these are all qualities we rightfully assign to our veterans.

Cornelius is a centurion, and that one title alone is enough to convey that this man is of upstanding character. "Centurions were chosen by merit, and so were men remarkable not so much for their daring courage as for their deliberation, constancy, and strength of mind."[42] Another commentary describes centurions as the "backbone of the Roman Army." Not chosen "so much as to be venturesome and daredevils as much as natural leaders, of steady and sedate spirit."[43]

I don't know about you, but these descriptions resonate with me. What strikes a chord with you regarding these descriptions?

Consistent and steady. These are the qualities of a man or woman I would respect enough to follow into battle. A man or woman who has earned the trust of not only his fellow soldiers and family, but God as well. He or she is a person of integrity. "The dictionary defines *integrity* as 'the state of being complete, unified.'" When I have integrity, my words and my deeds match up. I am who I am, no matter where I am or who I am with."[44]

And integrity is precisely what Christ calls us to.

42 Matthew G. Easton, *Easton's Bible Dictionary* (New York: Harper and Brothers, 1897).

43 Craig S. Keener, Matthew: The IVP New Testament Commentary Series (Downers Grove, Ill.: Intervarsity Press, 1997).

44 John C. Maxwell, *Developing the Leader Within You* (Thomas Nelson), p. 35. Kindle Edition.

Let's answer a few questions about ourselves as honestly as we can. Let's rate ourselves from "I do this well" to "I need work on this." Circle the one that you feel best describes you right now.

Are you devout, which is described as "reverence exhibited especially in actions," and God-fearing?[45]

I do this well　　　*I do this sometimes*　　　*I need to work on this*

Do you give generously to those in need?

I do this well　　　*I do this sometimes*　　　*I need to work on this*

Do you pray regularly?

I do this well　　　*I do this sometimes*　　　*I need to work on this*

Do you have a steady and sedate spirit?

I do this well　　　*I do this sometimes*　　　*I need to work on this*

Jesus tells a parable in the Gospel of Luke about a master and his servants. The master goes out for a while to a wedding banquet and the servants are left behind to their own devices. The question Jesus poses to his listeners is, would it be better when the Master returns to find his servants watching and ready for his arrival or for him to find them distracted and inattentive? To bring it into today's context, if your boss happens to drop by unexpectedly is it better for he or she to find you buried in your work or asleep and drooling? The answer is obvious, isn't it? The next question, which follows logically, is when your boss is looking to hand out the next big assignment whom are they more likely to give it to: the person who fell asleep or the person diligently working? Jesus closes this parable with a phrase that is often quoted, "From everyone who has been given much, much will be demanded; and from the one who has been entrusted with much, much more will be asked." (Luke 10:48b NIV) It's a life principle we are familiar with. If you prove yourself faithful with the smaller less important tasks you are often granted greater responsibility with the larger more significant ones.

This is certainly how it played out for Cornelius. He was faithful to what I like to label a person's *general calling*. When I say general calling, I am referring to certain distinct

---

45　James Strong, LLD, STD, *Strong's Expanded Exhaustive Concordance of the Bible* (Nashville: Thomas Nelson Publications, 2010), p. 1252.

qualities and practices that must be pursued by any and all who consider themselves a Christ-follower. Regardless of our personal and individual "I have to," we all have a unified general calling. Cornelius is a man of steadfast character, devout and God-fearing, always ready to give to those in need, and in prayer daily. These characteristics are qualities we all should be driven to imitate, whether we are in vocational ministry or the marketplace. Whether we are called to be president of the United States or to stay at home with our kids. All of us must seek to inhabit our general calling appropriately, and in a way marked by the life and teaching of Jesus.

Micah 6:8 gives us further great insight into our general calling. What are the three things in this passage that God has shown us to be *good*?

1. _____Act justly_____

2. _____love mercy_____

3. _____walk humbly_____

It is no coincidence that God chooses Cornelius for a mission that is of utmost importance to the future of His people and His church. What is that mission (see Acts 10:28)?

Cornelius has a vision in which an angel of the Lord appears to him. His first response to this divine appearance shouldn't surprise anyone in light of his character. "What is it, Lord?" Cornelius asks. Although we aren't told explicitly, I read a great deal of humility and submissiveness into his tone. A sort of "whatever you need, Lord, I will do" attitude. And then the angel says something quite interesting. Complete this sentence.

"Your prayers and gifts to the poor have come up as a _____ *offering before God"* (Acts 10:4).

The word *memorial* used here is defined as "that which keeps the memory of someone or something alive."[46] When we hold faithful to our general calling, our lives point to a larger reality that Jesus called the kingdom of God. In this realm, which exists within our current reality, love guides every decision, humility is strength, and victories are won not with a sword but with sacrifice.

---

46 Strong, *Strong's Expanded Exhaustive Concordance of the Bible*, p. 1252.

Our faithfulness to our general calling becomes a sign or memorial to God that we are up to the task. We have proved worthy of a new assignment, and it is here that our "I have to" is born. Cornelius has stepped up to this moment in time. He's not only going to witness, but also participate in, an unparalleled paradigm shift in the ministry of Peter and every single disciple to follow. I am convinced this role was birthed from a steady commitment to his general calling.

How can you be faithful to your general calling today as you await your next assignment?

Day 2: It's OK to Ask
I Samuel 10:1–11

Yesterday we discussed a principle that Jesus sums up in the story he told that is often called The Parable of the Shrewd Manager (Luke chapter sixteen). Obviously, being the Son of God, He said it much better than any of us ever could: "Whoever can be trusted with very little can also be trusted with much" (Luke 16:10). When we prove that we can be trusted with our general calling (and this is no small or insignificant task), we prove we can be trusted with more. And sometimes we discover that the "more" is equally exhilarating and terrifying. Have you ever felt called to something that both exhilarated and terrified you? If so, write about that time here.

Has your calling ever made you feel like you were in over your head? Have you wondered why in the world God chose you and then attempted to draw His attention to that person over there who was clearly more qualified for the job? Have you ever wondered what you got yourself into? Perhaps questioned God's sovereignty and decision-making ability? I am willing to bet all my savings that Saul, the first king of Israel, our character of focus for today, felt *all* of that. Read 1 Samuel 10:1. What was Saul stepping into that might have made him answer yes to all the preceding questions?

The first king of the nation of Israel. No big deal, right? (Of course, that question was laced with sarcasm!) But Saul did have a few things working in his favor. He is "as handsome as a young man that could be found anywhere in Israel," and he is also described as being "a head taller than anyone else" (I Samuel 9:2). His stature and appearance are certainly only going to accentuate his reputation with the people. Even still, this role of ruler for which Saul is being anointed is certain to be recorded in the history books, and all eyes will be on him. No pressure or anything!

With that in mind, it's no wonder God sends all kinds of confirming signs to Saul. When our "I have to" feels like we are about to bungie-jump off a cliff with only a chord standing between us and the rocky ravine bottom below, sometimes we need a shove! As in, we need another person willing to step in and push us off the edge if it comes to that! Because here is the thing: the last time I checked, God isn't physically present with us. Present, yes, but I wasn't able to stroll hand in physical hand with Him on my evening walk last night, and I didn't physically converse with Him over a Starbuck's latte this morning. (At this point, those kinds of moments have only happened in my dreams.)

My point is, sometimes we need a flesh-and-blood person, someone we can lock eyes with, someone we trust and who God entrusts to us, to be our sounding board and measure of sanity. God is more than attuned to what we need, and that's why I believe He uses people as one of the principle ways, other than His Word itself, through which we receive confirming signs.

Read 1 Samuel 10:2–11 and make a list of all the people Samuel, speaking on behalf of God, says Saul will encounter on his way.

1. 1 Samuel 10:2

2. 1 Samuel 10:3, 4

3. 1 Samuel 10:5

These people become necessary signs of confirmation for Saul. One commentator wrote, "If kingship is going to be more than a role, hung on him like a suit of ill-fitting clothes, he needs confirmation that there is more to this than Samuel's action, more in it than Samuel's bright idea. If Saul is, in fact, God's king, he needs more than Samuel's word for it before it becomes public. And that is what he gets: circumstantial signs that will validate Samuel's action, and a deep change within him that makes it possible to understand himself in God's terms, not his own."[47]

47 Eugene H. Peterson, *First and Second Samuel* (Westminster Bible Companion) (Presbyterian Publishing Corporation). Kindle Edition.

We are going to spend tomorrow talking about how a change in Saul's heart became another critical sign of confirmation. For now, let's reflect on our own journey. Has God ever used someone, perhaps something they said or did, as a confirming sign for you? Write about that experience or those experiences here.

As Michael and I prayed about leaving our home church to birth a new faith community, we asked God for confirming signs. This call for us was and is the "jump off a cliff" moment I described above. If we were going to leave the safety, security, and church family that knew us, in many ways better than we even knew ourselves, we were going to need some substantial and tangible affirmation. And that is exactly what we got. We had all kinds of conversations that were far from coincidence in light of what we had been praying. People would approach us and say, before there was any way they could know what we were feeling led toward: "You know, if you go anywhere [as in, leave the church], I am going with you." Others said, "I'm not sure what it is, but you're working through something significant right now, aren't you?" These kinds of comments became a theme of conversation during the weeks and months in which we were praying and fasting intentionally about our "I have to."

Just a few weeks ago I signed up for a women's retreat in which I knew no one. Nada. Not a soul. I'm not exactly an extrovert, so the idea of two days surrounded by not one previously known friend wasn't super enticing to me. Of course, I was sure in my spirit the answer to whether to attend was a yes. I signed up, resolved to be obedient, and then . . . I vacillated, as we often do when asked to venture outside our comfort zone. I then received this text from a friend of mine. Keep in mind, I hadn't told anyone except my husband about my situation. The text read: "Hey, how are you? Had you put on my heart today. Just praying for any big decision you may have coming up, and feel like the Lord wants you to know that He wants you to feel at peace about it. That no matter what you choose He has plans to prosper you and that you can't go wrong . . . feel at ease about saying yes . . . does that make sense?"

Our tendency at times is to write these kinds of experiences off to coincidence. But I believe they are far from that. Back to Saul: he is told by Samuel to expect three signs. "The first two, meeting the two men at Rachel's tomb and the three men at the oak of Tabor, are circumstantial and seemingly random, arbitrary even. But they will convey to Saul that Samuel's anointing and blessing was not an isolated act—there's a lot more going on here than 'Saul.' God works comprehensively, interconnectedly."[48] God does not make mistakes. Of course, trusting Him when we don't see the full picture, but only a fraction of it, is challenging.

What is God asking you to trust Him with today? Do you need to say yes to something that is outside your comfort zone? Are you dragging your feet when you know you need to pick them up and march on? If so, pray. Ask God to send you signs. This passage of Scripture affirms that it's OK to ask God for specific confirmation. So ask him! Ask for conversations, phone calls, texts, emails, sermons, podcasts, or whatever it might be that will help you in the discernment process. As you do, be sure to journal the ways in which you sense God's leading. Venturing into the new territory in which our "I have to" may lead us is intimidating. OK, let's get real: it's terrifying. But when we can look back and see that all signs point *this* direction, all arrows indicate *this* path, we gain confidence in our footing, find courage, and put an extra spring in our step.

So, let's do this.

---

48 Eugene H. Peterson, *First and Second Samuel* (Westminster Bible Companion) (Presbyterian Publishing Corporation). Kindle Edition.

Day 3: A Change of Heart
Mark 9:20–29 and 1 Samuel 10:7–13

I don't know about you, but yesterday's Scripture helped me catch my breath. I'm not sure why, but sometimes I feel like it's *not* OK to need a thousand confirming signs before I actually do what I am feeling called to do. Maybe it's because in my mind I feel I shouldn't need even the hundredth sign because sign three should have been enough! And if I'm really honest, I'm not sure how much room there is for doubt in my faith journey. Can you identify?

In Mark chapter nine, we read a story in which Jesus meets a father, a man desperate to find healing for his son, who has been suffering from all kinds of convulsions since childhood. The father has tried everything. Ever doctor, every healer, and every healing technique, but nothing has worked. Jesus is his last-ditch effort, and this man is desperate, and rightfully so, which is why he says, "*If* you can do anything, take pity on us and help us" (emphasis added). When you are at the end of your rope, and all hope is seemingly lost, you are prone to speak in terms of *ifs*. So let's read Mark 9:20–29. What does the father shout out in Mark 9:24?

It's such a relief to know I don't have to be the picture of perfect faith all of the time. It's OK to doubt, and it's OK to air out that doubt to Jesus. Jesus isn't offended by it; in fact, he embraces it as if to say, "Alright, now that we have that out of the way, let the healing begin." The father's admission of his unbelief actually ignites Jesus' restorative plans as opposed to squelching them. Whew!

Now that we have that off our chests, let's pick up again with the story of Saul that we started yesterday. Yesterday we read of all the people God used as part of Saul's confirmation. Go back and look at that section if it will help.

God uses more than just a few people as a sign for Saul, and not only that, He chooses to use specific descriptions of what Saul will encounter along the way. In regard to the men headed to Bethel, "One will be carrying three young goats, another three loaves of bread, and another a skin of wine." The attention to detail is pretty remarkable. There will be no mistaking that when Saul interacts with those three men, they are in fact the ones described to him by Samuel.

There is one more sign Samuel employs to tell Saul what he can expect. What is it? (Hint: read again 1 Samuel 10:6.)

Michael and I experienced a certain "change of heart" in those months of fasting and prayer that I described yesterday. I've written of the deep love we had for our home church several times, but I've not fully elaborated on just how profoundly and deeply we care for the staff. Rarely in ministry do you have the unique pleasure of serving alongside people who are not merely fellow workers, but actually dear friends. And so one evening as we gathered as a team socially, Michael and I collectively felt a shift in our spirits. We looked around the room at each person present, each and every individual who we loved so tenderly, and we heard a whisper: "It's OK to let go." It was as if, up until that very moment, we had our hands and our hearts tightly clenched on this specific church and these specific people, and God was now imploring us to loosen the grip. You can't embrace what is to come unless your hands are open to receiving it. That night our posture changed, and our church planting "I have to"— which until then had seemed abstract and obscure—came within grasp.

WHEN THE SPIRIT OF GOD COMES UPON US, WE FIND OURSELVES CAPABLE OF THINGS WE NEVER DREAMED POSSIBLE. OUR FEAR GETS DISPLACED BY THE COURAGE THAT COMES FROM KNOWING WE HAVE POWER FROM ABOVE.

Can you recall a time in which God changed your heart about something or someone? Describe it below.

It's fascinating how your heart and mind can be set on one thing one day, and before you know it, your desires and passions have shifted and landed on something else entirely. We have very dear friends whom we have done ministry with and alongside for the last ten years. About five years ago they sensed a call on their lives to leave their hometown, Phoenix, and plant a church in a suburb outside Dallas. They spent a few years there and endured all kinds of struggles; of course, there were joys as well. But it was challenging for them to begin a new faith community in a land, Texas, that was in many ways foreign to them. They might as well have gone to Beirut; at least, they said, it felt that way at times. Who knew two states so geographically close could be so different culturally!

They've since returned to the valley and found their niche in ministry closer to home, but we witnessed their journey, all the victories and defeats included. Which is why Michael said to me, on more than one occasion, "I will never plant a church." Well, God certainly has a sense of humor, because, at the time I write this, we now find ourselves less than two months away from launching our own church plant.

God changed our hearts in more ways than one. Our friends and family have often wondered, and asked us: "What happened?" Or, "What changed?" We don't have a great answer other than, "God. "God is what happened." And God is in fact what happens to Saul. You'll find the description of all that unfolds in 1 Samuel 10:7–13. Read it now, and let's step through the questions below.

What happens when Saul and his servant arrive in Gibeah? (10:10)

Similar to what was said of my husband and me, what was said about Saul by the prophets? (10:11)

Those who knew Saul before hardly recognized him. Something spectacular had happened to him; his heart had been transformed. Walter Brueggemann describes what took place this way:

"Saul becomes filled with energy and freedom beyond himself. The narrative strains to find words adequate for the new reality. This is the gift of the spirit. It is the power of God that works a newness in the face of established structures, order, and assumptions. Saul, by the work of the Spirit, is a genuine newness in Israel. The monarchy, so the text asserts, is not a human mechanism but rests in the inexplicable, un-administered power of God."[49]

When the Spirit of God comes upon us, we find ourselves capable of things we never dreamed possible. Our fear gets displaced by the courage that comes from knowing we have power from above. Have you ever had this kind of experience? One in which you found strength you didn't know and the ability to face the demands of the moment? If so, describe it below. If not, do you believe tapping into power greater than your own might alter how you view the challenges and obstacles in your path? Write about those feelings.

As you continue this journey of discerning your "I have to," continue asking God to reveal His confirming signs.

---

49 Walter Brueggemann, *First and Second Samuel: Interpretation: A Bible Commentary for Teaching and Preaching* (Presbyterian Publishing Corporation). Kindle Edition.

Day 4: A Collision of "I Have To's"
Acts 10:9–20, 21–47

A few months ago I sat down over coffee with a woman I had never met. We had been connected by a mutual friend who felt we should meet. We didn't know why. That is, until we started sharing our stores. My new friend was involved with a local ministry that existed to connect women with each other and with God. The ministry was birthed out of a realization that there are so many women feeling disconnected, lonely, and hurt. There had to be a way to bring women together in the name of Jesus, one that existed outside of any church, and therefore, outside of any preconceived notions of religion. Deep down, we know that the church was created to serve a necessary and beautiful purpose. But with imperfect people at the forefront of her leadership, wounds and hurt sometimes are inflicted, erecting barriers that block the wounded from ever returning through her doors. I fell in love with this ministry immediately, and even more so with the hearts of those in its leadership. Their mission struck such a deep chord with me because my passions aligned so completely with theirs. My new friend and I had no idea what God had in store for this newly formed friendship and partnership, but we *knew* our meeting had been ordained. Our two "I have to's" had collided, and we determined we were going to wait in expectation for what God would do with our alliance.

Our biblical text for today involves a similar collision of "I have to's." Let's begin by observing the two individuals whose paths cross. First we will examine their distinct and individual callings, and this will then allow greater insight into why God orchestrated the merging of their paths.

We will begin with a familiar man; he served as the focus of our lesson in day one of this week. Go back and briefly review the story of Cornelius.

God comes to Cornelius in a vision. What does He ask of him? (Acts 10:4–6)

God not only gives Cornelius a vision; He gives one to Peter as well. Next read what God communicates to Peter in Acts 10:9–16. Now, this story seems like the kind of crazy middle-of-the-night dreams I have in which unlikely and strange events occur, happenings having seemingly very little meaning. This vision, however, is quite the opposite; it is filled with meaning for Peter. This vision will be the catalyst for a radical paradigm shift carrying deep meaning for the ministry of Peter and all the apostles. Ultimately, this dream will have significant ramifications that will ripple through and reach our present day.

To bring some context, there are all manner of laws within the Jewish Torah that outline certain foods as "unclean" and therefore forbidden (Leviticus 11). "These food laws served to mark out the Jewish people from their non-Jewish neighbors, a rule reinforced by the prohibition on Jews eating with non-Jews."[50] With that in mind, what is God trying to communicate to Peter through his rooftop vision on this day?

It's confusing, isn't it? Especially for us today, people who are so far removed from Jewish culture and law. But I would argue it was just as confusing and strange for Peter as it is for us today. Eventually, he understands the vision's meaning: "I now realize how true it is that God does not show favoritism but accepts from every nation the one who fears and does what is right" (Acts 10:24). But it's only through the collision of his "I have to" with Cornelius's "I have to" that Peter receives this revelation. Clarity arrives. But it only comes through the crisscrossing of these two lives brought together by God, who is the master networker.

Read Acts 10:17. When did the men sent by Cornelius arrive?

Some timing God has, right? If you're ever wondering if God is at work, stand back and observe the timing of how the events of your near or distant past unfolded. That phone call or text at the exact right moment, that detour you were forced to take, the routine examination that caught cancer just in time. There's no question He is behind it all.

---

50 N.T. Wright, Dale Larsen, Sandy Larsen, *Acts (N. T. Wright for Everyone Bible Study Guides).* (Intervarsity Press). Downers Grove, Illinois. Kindle Edition.

And God doesn't stop with the arrival of Cornelius' men. If there was any question as to whether these servants were sent as a confirmation or a distraction, the answer is made undeniably clear to Peter. How?

Fill in the blanks from Acts 10:19, 20.

> *While Peter was _____ thinking about the vision, The Spirit said to him, "Simon, three men are looking for you. So get up and go downstairs. Do not _____ to go with them, for I have sent them"* (Acts 10:19, 20).

Is it not so obvious that God's hand is at work? Can you recall a time in which you had this kind of experience? One in which there was no mistaking that God was meticulously orchestrating even the most minute details so He could draw you onto His path and place you in the center of His plans? If so, write about such a time here.

Let's take a moment to examine some of the reasons God might have hand-selected these two individuals for this particular assignment. Fill in the following chart with some of the characteristics or descriptions of both Cornelius and Peter that indicate why their partnership was necessary to the overall success of the mission. I've included some Scripture references to get us started, and left an extra line to perhaps find more crisscrossing character traits. (Hint: great spots to find more clues to Peter's heart and character are the books of 1 Peter and 2 Peter.)

	Peter	**Cornelius**	
Acts 2:14			Acts 10:1
1 Peter 1:1			Acts 10:2
Galatians 2:8			Acts 10:22

Now answer these questions.

Was Cornelius a Jew or Gentile?

Was Cornelius liked or disliked by the Jews?

Would Peter, being both a witness to Jesus and an apostle, have the kind of authority necessary to communicate the new revelation of God made known through the vision?

Would the crowds be likely to hear what Peter has to say, or disregard it?

With all this in mind, why did God chose these two men to be the mouthpiece for His desire that Jews and Gentiles both be saved?

Whew! I know this has been a lot of thought, but now that you have been diligent and completed it, I think your reward will come as you read the rest of this story.

Now read Acts 10:21–47. It's a beautiful conclusion, isn't it?

Allow me to share a modern-day parable to give us insight into what is unfolding within this text.

You open the mail one day and find an invitation. A new friend has decided to host a dinner party and you're on the guest list. You can't wait—Martha Stewart has nothing on your friend—and so you know that everything from the food to the flowers will be nothing short of perfection. You can't wait; you are beside yourself with excitement. As the days pass and the party inches closer, you wonder, who will be there? Your friend hobnobs with the elite of society, so the guest list is sure to be bursting with everyone who is anyone.

Finally the day arrives. You put on your very best, spend extra time on your hair and makeup, and wear your new shoes, the ones that were unconscionably overpriced and yet you swore you would one day need! You arrive fashionably late, the first rule in how to make a grand entrance at a social event. You make your appearance, draped on your date's arm, looking fabulous, sure that all eyes will be on you. But as your eyes scan the room you are filled with shock and horror. There before your eyes is the hospital's neurosurgeon standing next to the neighborhood homeless guy! You recognize the woman seated next to you as the strung-out drive-thru attendant. The whole room is filled with these kinds of peculiar pairings. CEOs and convenient store workers, TV personalities and teachers, entrepreneurs and garbage men. The rich intermingled with the poor, the prestigious commingling with the common. All lines that separate have suddenly become blurred over a table shared and the breaking of bread.

You steal a moment away with your new friend. "This is quite a group. Not really what I expected," you say, trailing off to leave her space for a response.

All you get is this: "Yes, quite a group indeed."

It's a parable. But even it, I doubt, would come close to the shock Peter experienced when confronted with the news that the Gospel message was not just for the Jews but the *whole world!* Gathered there that historic day are Gentiles and Jews alike, friends and family of Cornelius and those allied with Peter—all rubbing elbows as Peter preaches. What comes out of Peter's mouth sends shock waves through the room. The good news is for all people. With Jesus at the center, all people are invited, and everyone is in.

"In Jesus the Messiah of Israel, God has broken down the barrier between Jews and Gentiles, humiliating both categories (Jews, because they apparently lost their privileged position; Gentiles, because they have to acknowledge the Jewish Messiah) in order to reveal God's mercy to both."[51]

God uses the crisscrossing of two "I have to's" to usher in a new movement. He is revealing the mystery that has been kept hidden for thousands of years. God is available and accessible to *all* people groups.

Imagine what would have happened if Cornelius had ignored the vision given to him? How would everything be different today if Peter had written off his dream as a strange and meaningless hallucination? What if these two men hadn't been obedient to their parts of the equation?

The truth is, when all signs point to "I have to," it's not always just for our sake. Sometimes there is a much greater plan about to unfold, and we are invited to participate. Sometimes our *yes* affects somebody else's.

Have you ever experienced a kind of overlapping of "I have to's" like Cornelius and Peter did? If so, write about it here, ending our time together today.

51 Wright, Larsen, Larsen, *Acts*. Kindle Edition.

Day 5: Charting the Signposts
1 Corinthians 12:12, 27; 1 Peter 4:10

Yesterday we spend some time unwrapping how God used two separate lives and two distinct "I have to's" to bring a mystery that had been kept secret for thousands of years to light. What mystery, you might ask? "This mystery is that through the gospel the Gentiles are heirs together with Israel, members together of one body, and sharers together in the promise in Christ Jesus" (Ephesians 3:6).

God took Peter, an apostle well respected by the Jews, and Cornelius, a highly esteemed Roman solder and Gentile, to reveal the truth. Through the perfectly designed intersection of two paths merged together through the very hand of God Himself, Peter reaches a revolutionary conclusion.

"I now realize how true it is that God does not show favoritism but accepts from every nation the one who fears him and does what is right" (Acts 10:34).

God is for *everyone*. And the reach of that *everyone* extends to all of us right here and right now.

As we closed yesterday's lesson, we pondered an important question that I would like to use as the starting point today. How would the circumstances have been different if either Peter or Cornelius had not responded in obedience to God's calling? We will never know the answer, but I would offer that such a decision would have radically changed the outcome. My point here is that the faithfulness you exhibit toward your "I have to" affects my capacity to be faithful to my "I have to." By God's design, the lives of His children were meant to be intrinsically intertwined. The apostle Paul writes, "Just as a body, though one, has many parts, but all its many parts form one body, so it is with Christ. Now you are the body of Christ, and each one of you is a part of it" (I Corinthians 12:12, 27).

Have you ever injured your toe? You never would have dreamed that such a small body part, one that at first glance seems ugly (don't be offended; I'm speaking strictly about my toes here!) and somewhat useless, would play such a critical role in the operation of the body as a whole. But when your toe hurts, you walk differently, and not immediately; over time, you find your other body parts—say your ankle or your knee—start to compensate for that toe. And then, with seemingly no notice, your back starts to hurt, which subsequently causes an extraordinarily uncomfortable crick in your neck. Several thousands of dollars later, after an inordinate amount of visits to the chiropractor, you discover the culprit was your big toe all along.

This is how it is in the body of Christ when one person fails to pull their weight. When just one person fails to seek out and discover their gifts or chooses to cast them aside for fear of failure, or through outright apathy, other people's "I have to's" are put in jeopardy. I'm not trying to put pressure or heap on guilt or anything of that sort. I just want all of us, including myself, to sense the gravity of our role and the disorder it can cause if we don't fulfill it.

> *Each of you should use whatever gift you have received to serve others, as faithful stewards of God's grace in its various forms* (1 Peter 4:10).

What does this verse mean to you? What is God speaking to you right now through His Word?

When we take our gifts and release them into the world, we become God's grace to someone. What a joy! What a blessing! And what a high responsibility!

I would like to reserve the rest of today for some deeper reflection. While I can't force you to participate in this exercise, I'd like to urge you, as strongly as I can, to do this.

So I want to ask you to lock yourself in the bathroom; closets work too! Wherever you need to go, shut yourself off from the world around you. Here are the rules:

No phone.
No TV.
No music.
No distractions.
Just your workbook and a lot of quiet.

Are you there yet? If it's impossible to get there now (I understand you have lives apart from this study!), mark out some time later in the day or tomorrow and guard that time with your life. Consecrate that time to this activity.

Now, quiet your mind. Take some deep breaths in and, while you do, imagine you are breathing in God's plans, His words, His will, what it is *He* wants to say. When you exhale, release everything that is vying for your attention other than God. Lay down your to-do list, your work responsibilities, your family concerns . . . breathe it all out. Imagine it all as a pile of dust on the floor and sweep it all away.

The next part is simple. And because it's simple, it's hard. Don't try to complicate it. Just ask God one question.

What are my signposts?

Let Him recall to your mind people He has placed in your path. Have there been text messages? Emails? Words over coffee spoken by a friend that now need to become His words to you?

Has He changed your heart recently? Has he fanned the flame of a passion toward a specific person, task, or ministry? Has he allowed a passion to die in anticipation of what is to come?

Be silent. And *listen.* If words come to your mind, write them down. If you are prompted to talk to God about something in particular, talk it out with Him just as you would with a friend or loved one. . . .

What is *He* saying? Remember, this moment is between you and God, so take as much or as little time as you feel led to.

I hope this week of study has brought your further from fear, from apathy, from intimidation, from insecurity, and closer to your "I have to."

Thank you for your diligence, dear friends. Can't wait to meet up again next week!

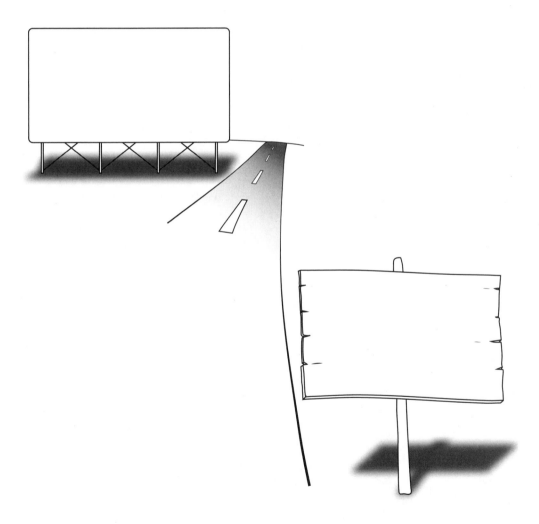

WHEN "I HAVE TO" MEANS: "I HAVE TO . . . WAIT"

The Setup

*W*ait. Just the sound of that word rolling off my tongue turns my stomach a bit and makes me clench up. *Wait* is defined by the dictionary as "to remain inactive or in a state of repose, as until something unexpected happens."[52] I would add to that definition: remaining inactive until something expected happens. Like waiting in line for a ride, a vacation, a promotion, or whatever it might be. Whether what you're waiting for is on your radar or in the furthest stratosphere of your mind, the process can feel torturous, can't it? And yet, it also often seems that at every turn in the road there lies another reason to wait. I'm speaking both literally and figuratively here. Perhaps you strive for months to get pregnant and then, once with child, you wait nine months before you get to meet your little one. You have an architect draw up a plan for your long-awaited home renovation and then wait for months before the project actually comes to fruition. You put a pot of water on the stove and wait for what seems like sixty minutes—in reality, six—for it to come to a boil. The list goes on and on. Hurry up and wait, and then hurry up and wait some more.

---

52 http://dictionary.reference.com

Remember when you were a kid and your life was just a series of activities or events to be waited for? . . . I can't wait until the weekend because I'm sleeping over at my friend's house. . . . I can't wait until next month because we're going on family vacation. . . . I can't wait until I'm ten because then I'll be in double digits! . . . I can't wait until I'm done with high school because it's so lame. You get my point. And now, as an adult, you're wondering what all the rush was about? Now, you wish you could tell time to slow down and it would actually listen to you!

What I'm realizing, at the ripe old age of thirty-two, is sometimes the sweetest moments lie in the waiting. We took our oldest two boys to New York City the week just before Halloween 2014. It was the trip of a lifetime, the kind you depart from with both the deep satisfaction that comes from knowing you gave it all you had, and then the acute depression that comes from knowing you will never be able to replicate the experience, not in a million years. We did it all: Rockefeller Center, ice skating in Central Park, FAO Schwarz, a boat cruise around the Statue of Liberty, Times Square, a Broadway show—you name it, we did it. Ask my boys what their favorite part was and they will most likely list off a few of the above activities, but they'll also tell you one of the highlights was riding the subway. This is in part because the NYC subway, for a couple of Phoenix-born boys, is an eye-opening and enthralling experience in and of itself. But it's also because when we rode the subway, we played all manner of games as a family. We were handcuffed to the moment, stuck together in the in-between, and forced to hold still and hold tight to each other.

So this week, we are going to talk about what happens when God calls you to do something and then makes you . . . wait. When the green light in front of you turns red and, for whatever reason—most of which we cannot know but for hindsight—your "I have to" becomes an "I have to wait."

Let's review these questions from week three of our personal study.

Day 1

1. Describe the character of Cornelius. Of all of his character traits, which do you identify with most? More specifically, which of his character traits do you hope to emulate in your life?

2. According to Micah 6:8, what practices encompass our *general calling*?

How can you be faithful to your general calling as you await your next assignment?

Day 2

1. Who did God send to Saul to help confirm his "I have to"?

Has God ever used people, perhaps something they said or did, as a confirming sign?

Day 3

1. How does knowing it's OK to ask for confirming signs allow you to breathe a sigh of relief?

What happens when Saul and his servant arrive in Gibeah? (See I Samuel 10:10.)

2. Have you ever experienced supernatural courage because of the Spirit of God in your life? Perhaps you found strength you didn't know you had and the ability to face the demands of the moment. If so, elaborate in the space below. If not, do you believe that tapping into power greater than your own might alter how you view the challenges and obstacles in your path?

Day 4

1. What does God ask of Cornelius? What happens in Peter's vision?

2. What do you think God is trying to communicate to Peter through this vision?

3. Have you had the kind of experience where there's no mistaking that God was meticulously orchestrating even the most minute details to draw you onto His path and place you in the center of His plans?

4. Have you ever experienced the kind of overlapping of "I have to's" that Cornelius and Peter did? If so, elaborate here.

Day 5

1. Read 1 Peter 4:10. What does this verse mean to you in this moment? What is God speaking to you through His Word?

Watch Session 4 at Christyfay.com: When All Signs Point to "I Have To"

WHEN "I HAVE TO" MEANS "I HAVE TO . . . WAIT"

Day 1: Character Is Honed in the Waiting
1 Samuel 16

In the Setup to this week we talked about how outright frustrating and tedious it can be to have to wait! There are very few people who enjoy the process, and yet there really is no getting around it. From waiting in line for a donut to waiting until the bell rings to waiting for the "right one" to finally make his or her appearance, it seems like there's always something we long for that's not yet within our grasp. There are no two men from the Bible more well-acquainted with this process of waiting than Abraham and David. And this makes them our point of study for this week. Our first two days will center around David and the last three around Abraham.

We spent some time last week looking at the journey of Saul and the events that led him to the throne of Israel. We are now going to fast-forward, five chapters in fact, in the story of Saul and David. (Feel free to read the five chapters in between for greater context and clarity.) There is one verse in those interceding five chapters that serves as a sort of Cliff's Notes. Turn to 1 Samuel 15:10, 11 and fill in these blanks.

Then the word of the Lord came to Samuel: "I regret that I have made Saul king, because he has _____ away from me and has not carried out my _____." Samuel was angry, and he cried out to the Lord all that night.

The Lord is fed up with Saul's continued disobedience and disregard for His ways, and He will not stand for it any longer. It's time for a new king to rise up and take His place. As He often does, God has a particular person in mind for this assignment. Let's read about who God selects as the new king of Israel in 1 Samuel 16. Though you already know who this person is, let's dig as deeply as we can into David's life.

Read 1 Samuel chapter 16, today's main text. Can you even imagine this scene? All of Jesse's sons lined up in a row, on display for the whole town of Bethlehem to see. Each of them believing and hoping that they will be the one chosen. Eliab nudges his brother Abinadab in the ribs, leaning over to whisper, "You know, I'm the strongest and best-looking of any of you riffraff. Surely this lot will be cast on me." Of course, to everyone's shock and dismay, none of the seven present are selected. Samuel turns to Jesse with lost eyes. "Are there any more?" he asks hesitantly. And before long in walks sweaty and disheveled youngest brother David, smelling like a bunch of sheep, no less. "This is the one," Samuel declares on behalf of God, and the crowd erupts with gasps. It's a fantastic story, and one we will examine in greater depth tomorrow. But for now, what's most important to know is that when this story unfolds, scholars believe, David was only between ten and thirteen years old.[53]

Now turn to 2 Samuel 5:4. How old was David when he finally gained control of the throne of Judah?

It could have been as many as twenty years between when David is anointed and when he actually becomes king. *Twenty years!* Talk about waiting. If you're like me, your first question is, *Why?* Why would God so clearly choose David for the throne, and then wait that long before allowing him to inhabit it? We often have that exact question about our circumstances, don't we? When our "I have to" becomes "I have to wait," it can feel as though we're that dog, the one chasing the bone that's dangling right in front our face, but just out of reach of our mouths. Sort of like we're on a wild goose chase with no goose in sight! We ask, "How long will you make us wait, Lord, for what you've promised?" And this is precisely what David wonders: "How long, Lord? Will you forget me forever? How long will you hide your face from me?" (Psalm 13:1). Why? We may not be able to answer this question about our lives, maybe not for years to come. Lucky for us, we know the end of David's story. Made clear to us through the pages of Scripture is the fruit produced in David's life, which came only through the season of waiting which he

---

53 William H. Gross, "Living Stone Class," Colorado Springs, Colorado. http://livingstonesclass.org/Archive/DavidChronologyGross.pdf 2005. Accessed January 13, 2016.

endured. God is up to something. He always is. We often just don't see the full picture. Charles Stanley wrote:

> God is changing hearts and engineering circumstances we have no idea even exist. Therefore, the delays we face are not a denial of His promises; rather an integral of His strategy to arrange all the details and get us positioned for His excellent plan.[54]

We're going to spend the rest of the day charting some of these preparatory events experienced by David and the fruit it produced in his life. Read the short synopsis I've provided in regard to that specific section of the story. Look up the verse or verses I've indicated and then fill in the blanks provided. Finally, write the lesson that you believe was being taught by God and the kind of fruit it might have produced in David's life.

1. The Israelites are in battle with the Philistines. Saul is camped on one side of the valley with the Israelite army; on the other side of the valley resides the Philistines. One man, one *very large* man, named Goliath, steps forward and calls out, "Choose a man and have him come down to me. If he is able to fight and kill me, we will become your subjects; but if I overcome him and kill him, you will become our subjects and serve us" (1 Samuel 17:9). Not one Israelite is brave enough to step forward with the exception of . . . none other than David, the runt of Jesse's sons. He is willing to take on this beast of a man without even a trace of armor, with only a few pebbles and a slingshot for a weapon.

   Now read 1 Samuel 17:45–47. Complete this sentence.

   "All those gathered here will know that it is not by sword or _____ that the Lord saves; for the battle is the _____, and he will give all of you into our hands" (1 Samuel 17:47).

   What potential lesson was learned by David, and what kind of fruit might have been produced by this experience?

2. King Saul hires David as one of his armor-bearers, and he begins to take quite a liking to this young man (1 Samuel 16:21). The two seem to be getting along well until, as the Scriptures indicate, an "evil spirit from God comes forcefully on Saul" (1 Samuel 17:10). While David is with Saul, playing the lyre as he often does, the

---

54 Charles F. Stanley, *Waiting on God* (New York: Howard Books, 2015).

king makes his first attempt to take the life of his so-called friend. And thus begins a long line of threats, and even several murder attempts, ordered by Saul. David is forced to flee and hide out wherever he can as the wild and violent king seeks to hunt him down.

Now read 1 Samuel 18:15, 16 and 1 Samuel 23:14 and complete these sentences.

Then Saul sent the men back to see David and told them, "Bring him up to me in his bed so that I may _____ him." But when the men entered, there was the idol in the bed, and at the head was some goats' hair (1 Samuel 18:15, 16).

David stayed in the wilderness strongholds and in the hills of the Desert of Ziph. Day after day Saul _____ for him, but God did not give David into his hands (1 Samuel 23:14).

What could David have learned from these experiences? What fruit might have been produced in his life as a result?

3. The game of cat and mouse continues. Saul hunts David down like a lion mercilessly tracking its prey. Although David is tired and exhausted, unable to be with friends and family and forced into hiding, God's hand of protection is on him, and the Lord preserves his life again and again. When Saul gets word that David is hiding out in the Desert of En Gedi, the king assembles three thousand young men to seek out and capture David and his men. Saul unknowingly makes his way into the very cave in which David and his men are camped. David now has his first opportunity to become the huntee instead of the hunted.

Read 1 Samuel 24:18, 19 to see what David does; fill in the blanks below.

"You have just now told me about the good you did to me; the Lord delivered me into your hands, but you did not kill me. When a man finds his enemy, does he let him get away _____? May the Lord reward you well for the way you _____ me today."

Only a few chapters later, David is once again confronted with an opportunity to take the life of Saul. Read 1 Samuel 26:5–12 to find out what he does. Fill in the blank from verse nine.

But David said to Abishai, "Don't destroy him! Who can lay a hand on the Lord's _____ and be guiltless?" (1 Samuel 26:9).

What lesson was God teaching? What kind of fruit might have been produced in David's life because of these two experiences?

We could spend so much time reading through these chapters in the book of 1 Samuel, the long period between David's anointing and when he finally takes the throne. (If you have time and feel so inclined, you should.) David endured so much in those years: his boss and father-in-law hated him, attempted to take his life, and forced him to run and hide for his life. Michal, Saul's daughter and David's wife, is forced to marry another man; two of his other wives are captured by Saul's men; his best friend is killed; and the list goes on. All manner of tragedy and intensely challenging circumstances brought David to his knees again and again. He cried out, "Do not turn me over to the desire of my foes, for false witnesses rise up against me, sprouting malicious accusation" (Psalm 27:12). And yet somehow, in spite of it all, he would also write, "I remain confident of this; I will see the goodness of the Lord in the land of the living" (Psalm 27:13).

What did David write in Psalm 27:14?

David is known as a "man after God's own heart" (1 Samuel 13:14). This is a title widely understood and accepted by biblical scholars, modern-day Jesus followers, and skeptics alike. But this all-too-famous character was not formed overnight. It came only in the waiting, in the dark moments, in the days he spent hiding in caves with only the Lord for a companion. God's plan was always to raise David up as king; God will not and cannot go back on his promise. As Victor Raymond Edman, a former president of Wheaton College, once said, "Delay never thwarts God's purpose; rather, it polishes God's instrument."[55] David would be king, and it would be upon David's throne that Jesus would eventually take His full and righteous reign (Luke 1:32).

---

55 Charles F. Stanley, *Waiting on God* (New York: Howard Books, 2015), p. 21.

Our dreams pale in comparison to those of Jesus. Our goals fall short of the many and spectacular ones He has planned. The story of our lives as told by us will never measure up to the story He has written. And still, often, we have to wait. The question remains: Can we trust Him to fulfill what He has promised even when the horizon looks bleak and hope has run out?

So, has your "I have to" ever become an "I have to wait"? Are you in a holding pattern at this point in life? Elaborate below.

What wisdom and insight gleaned from David's story can help you with your journey today?

What kind of seeds does God want to plant now for the plentiful harvest He has planned for the future? What kind of fruit do you hope to see produced?

Day 2: Clothing of Consecration
Joshua 3:5, 14-17; Exodus 28:1–4

After I gave birth to my third child, Crosby, I knew I wanted one more. Four was the number God intended for our family; in my heart I knew it. Of course, I certainly wasn't ready at that exact moment to plunge into another pregnancy. Later, when the time was right, we began trying. Now, I have to preface this story by saying that with my first two pregnancies, Michael and I conceived in the very first month. So, when it came to this particular arena of my life, I wasn't used to waiting. Fertile Myrtle here seemed to have no problems becoming "with child," as the Scriptures put it. So when one month passed and the pregnancy test read negative, I thought, *That's strange.* Then another month passed: negative again. I began thinking, *What's wrong? This isn't normal.* I know, I know: this stream of thought after a mere two months is nothing short of ridiculous. Trust me, I know it now, and I knew it then, too. Those of you who've waited years and years to get pregnant and may even find out you will never carry a child in your physical body want to hit me over the head with a frying pan, and rightfully so. I confess I was being obscenely unreasonable about the whole thing. It takes most people an average of six months to conceive, so the fact it took us three was still fast-paced, according to the norm. But it didn't feel that way to me.

I remember one afternoon I called my mom. And, as often happens, my unruly and totally unwarranted emotions bled out all over that conversation. "What if I can't get pregnant?" (And this was a real fear since my mom had me, and then couldn't have any more children.) "What if something is wrong?" . . . "I know I'm becoming completely silly, but God told me my number was four, so why am I not pregnant?" . . . Well, Mom talked me down from a ledge and somehow gracefully made me feel like I wasn't crazy. I'll never forget when I hung up the phone, I looked upward and said, "Alright, God. Enough of this nonsense. I know it's a lot to ask when I already have three healthy and incredible children. But one more would be great. If you don't mind, that is. But, in the end, I've decided to trust you know what is best for this family far more than I do."

Nine months later, we welcomed our fourth. And wow, was God s plan better than anything I could have conjured up on my own. Not only did He give me a healthy baby, he gave us our girl. She is pure gift and the most perfect completion to this family. The cherry on top of an already unbelievable ice cream sundae.

My point here is that even the short wait I endured forced me to deeper places of trust in Him. I came face to face with a question that has and always will haunt all of us that profess to be God-followers: Christy, do you believe I have your best interests in mind? I knew the answer to that question in theory, but when it clashed with my best version of reality, my true convictions were put to the test.

Do you believe God has your best interests in mind? Why or why not? Don't shy away from a truthful answer, even if it's one you don't think is the "right answer."

I promised yesterday that we would come back to David's story today, specifically the part in which he is chosen and anointed as the next king of Israel. For a quick refresher, reread 1 Samuel 16:12, 13.

What did Samuel do to David with the horn of oil?

Anointing is a somewhat strange concept for us today. You may come from a church tradition in which this practice is common, or from one in which it's rarely performed. Or you may not come from a church tradition at all, in which case this ritual is probably quite foreign. I've most frequently seen anointing oil used at infant or child dedications; the pastor smears a small amount on the baby's forehead as an act of consecration. What does it all mean? The Hebrew word for *anoint* is *mashach*, and it means "to consecrate." In the Old Testament the word *anoint* is most often used to indicate a special laying aside or setting a part of a person for a specific office or function.[56]

Now let's turn to Joshua 3. Fill in the blanks of Joshua 3:5.

Joshua told the people, "Consecrate yourselves, for tomorrow the Lord will do _____ things among you."

What amazing things was Joshua referring to? (Hint: read ahead to Joshua 3:14–17.)

---

56 James Strong, LLD, STD, *Strong's Expanded Exhaustive Concordance of the Bible* (Nashville: Thomas Nelson Publications, 2010), 4886.

The word *consecrate* has a similar meaning as anoint. The Hebrew word here is *qudesh*, which is defined as "to pronounce or observe as clean." Much like anoint, the "word is used in some form or another to represent being set apart for the work of God."[57]

We see it first mentioned in Exodus 28:1–4. Go ahead and read those verses.

This reading takes us to the middle of the book of Exodus, in a section in which God is giving specific instructions in regard to the tabernacle, or tent of meeting. The greater story being unfolded in this particular book of the Torah (the first five books of the Bible) is one of rescue and delivery. Moses has led God's people, the Israelites, out of the land of Egypt and therefore out from under the hand of enslavement that has held them captive for hundreds of years. Moses and the Israelites are now wandering in the desert. Of course, God makes it clear that they are not alone: feeding them with manna (Exodus 16:35), quenching their thirst with water from a rock (17:6), teaching them the way in which they are to live with the Ten Commandments (Exodus 20), and guiding them with a pillar of cloud by day and a pillar of fire by night (13:21). And if God is so clearly with them, the question becomes, Where is He to dwell? The tabernacle became that sacred sanctuary the Israelites kept and carried with them while journeying through the desert. It was home to the tablets inscribed with the Ten Commandments Moses had brought down with him from Mount Sinai. "Moses would go into the Tent and the pillar of cloud would come down and hover outside, showing the divine presence, while God spoke with Moses."[58]

That gives us some background. Now back to the section of verses we just read from Exodus 28.

Who is it that will serve as priests? (v. 1)

For what purpose are the skilled workers to make garments for Aaron?

What kind of garments were they to make? List them here.

---

57 James Strong, LLD, STD, *Strong's Expanded Exhaustive Concordance of the Bible* (Nashville: Thomas Nelson Publications, 2010), 6942.

58 John Bowker, *The Complete Bible Handbook* (New York: D.K. Publishing, 1998), p. 53.

If you continue to read through this chapter, you see descriptions of each of the garments and specific instructions on the materials to be used and how each item is to be constructed. I can only imagine how many hours it took for the skilled workers to create all of these elaborate articles of clothing. Why? The Scriptures give a clear answer, and although we have already covered it, for the sake of emphasis, fill in the following blank from Exodus 28:3.

> *"Tell all the skilled workers to whom I have given wisdom in such matters that they are to make garments for Aaron, for his consecration, _____ _____ _____ serve me as priest"* (Exodus 28:3).

If Aaron is to go into the presence of God to minister before Him directly,[59] then he must be set apart; he *has* to be consecrated.

We no longer operate under the same system as Moses and the Israelites. We don't have a tabernacle where the presence of God resides because, with Jesus, a new system, or covenant, was birthed. "Don't you know that you yourselves are God's temple and that God's Spirit dwells in your midst?" (1 Corinthians 3:16). "You are royal priests, a holy nation, God's very own possession" (1 Peter 2:9, *NLT*). The reality is this: We are all "Aaron's" now, so we all must wear garments of consecration. Of course, ours will look a little different then his.

As "God's very own possession," what does Colossians 3:12 say about the kind of clothing we are to wear? Make a list below.

Of the qualities you listed, are there any that are produced quickly, or is this kind of character only formed with time?

Romans 5:4 says, "And endurance develops strength of character, and character strengthens our confident hope of salvation."

What develops strength of character? Circle and underline the word in the verse above and then meditate on this statement from God.

59 David Guzik, *Verse by Verse Commentary Exodus* (Santa Barbara, California: Enduring Word Media, 2012).

I can envision those skilled Hebrew workers now . . . heads bent over, focused, as they engrave in gold filigree the names of each of the sons of Israel like a seal on the breastpiece. They gather the fine jewels and, ever so delicately, even meticulously, sew them into the hem of the robe of the ephod. Hours and hours stretch into long days and even longer months. Perhaps their fingers grow raw to the bone from the painstaking work before them. But they refuse to quit, their determination rises, and this is because, in the end, they recognize it's all worth it. This is what is required for Aaron to be consecrated and readied for the work of God.

We have a Master at work on us as well, one skilled in His craft. One who has committed to sew in us a heart of compassion. To stitch into the very fabric of our lives kindness and humility, and to hem us in with gentleness and patience. His work is steady, but it's not always fast. "For we are God's masterpiece," Paul writes in his letter to the church at Ephesus. "He has created us anew in Christ Jesus." And why has He done such a thing? Paul continues: "So we can do the *good things* he planned for us long ago" (Ephesians 2:10, *NLT*, emphasis added).

We have many good things planned out for us. Our God has fashioned and formed many an "I have to" for each and every one of us—enough to fill a lifetime. But if we hope to inhabit these, we must be set apart. And the work of consecration can only happen over time.

MY POINT HERE IS THAT EVEN THE SHORT WAIT I ENDURED FORCED ME TO DEEPER PLACES OF TRUST IN HIM.

The people of Israel were given an unbelievably great and grand calling.

"God's presence in the tabernacle is a statement about God's intended presence in the entire world. The glory manifest there is to stream out into the larger world. The shining of Moses' face in the wake of the experience of the divine glory (see 34:29–35) is to become characteristic of Israel as a whole, a radiating out into the larger world of those glorious effects of God's dwelling among Israel. As a kingdom of priests (see 19:5, 6), they have a role of mediating this glory to the entire cosmos."[60]

And now that high calling—"mediating this glory to the entire cosmos"—rests on our shoulders. We are the priests and our bodies the tabernacle. Have your ever heard anything more wonderful and altogether awe-inspiring in your entire life? Of course, directly following the wonder comes the realization of the profound responsibility and unequaled burden that comes with the title. It's the greatest job that ever has or ever will be handed out.

As we close today, dear friends, let me reassure you: If your "I have to" has transformed into an "I have to wait," it's well worth that wait.

---

60 Terence E. Fretheim, *Exodus: Interpretation: A Bible Commentary for Teaching and Preaching* (Westminster John Knox Press). Kindle Edition. Pp. 271–272.

Day 3: Abiding Versus Striving
Genesis 12:1–3

I love Christmas, don't you? It really is the most wonderful time of the year. After I've put the Halloween costumes away, I know I can start the countdown. How many days before I can drag those big red bins out from the storage closet, the ones jam-packed with ornaments, garland, nativity scenes, and Christmas lights? When I can just let loose? I know, most people wait until Thanksgiving. But I've found that waiting that long cramps my Christmas decorating style. So, in an attempt to avoid my husband thinking I am crazier than I already am, I wait—painstakingly, I might add—until the weekend before Thanksgiving, and then I go to town. Which means I crank up Bing Crosby singing, "I'm Dreaming of a White Christmas"(which is definitely in our dreams here in Phoenix, Arizona) and my Christmas bins begin throwing up all over my house. It's awesome.

At least, in theory it's awesome. Every year, as the time arrives, I mistakenly believe that all four of my children will angelically help unpack every single decoration and find that perfect place for them in our home. I slip *Elf* or *How the Grinch Stole Christmas* in the DVD player and light a fire. And we all work together, for about twenty minutes, or at least until something much more exhilarating than decorating the Christmas tree captures their attention and they disappear into the playroom. Hours later, I'm still there, back nearly broken from bending over the stupid bins, pulling out decorations, shirt soaked in sweat, and cursing my ceilings, which forced me to buy that ten-foot Christmas tree. Because, let's face it, decorating for Christmas isn't all fun and candy canes, is it? It's hard work.

It's in these moments I look out my window at our neighbor's fruit tree, branches stretching up and over the wall in plain sight, and I think: If only decorating the Christmas tree was as easy as oranges blooming on a fruit tree. I think that's why the Bible asserts that we should attempt to model our lives more after fruit trees than Christmas trees. "Remain in me, as I also remain in you. No branch can bear fruit by itself; it must remain in the vine. Neither can you bear fruit unless you remain in me" (John 15:4). It's less about decorating and more about remaining. And remaining takes a lot of waiting. Fruit isn't produced overnight. It takes time, good soil conditions, water, and a whole lot of other stuff too. But if we wait on Him while remaining in Him, our lives become just like a fruitful tree, the kind with so many oranges to go around that everyone we meet can take one and there are still tons left over.

Of course, sometimes I prefer the faster route and, like decorating a Christmas tree, I attempt to shove fruits of the Spirit—like kindness, compassion, and gentleness—all up over my branches. But it's hard work, and all too quickly I find my efforts in vain and those fruits, like ornaments, scattered all over the hypothetical floor of my life.

This is precisely what we talked about in day one of this week's study. David remained in God, trusting His plan and purposes, and in the time of waiting fruit began to bloom in his life. He could have forced his way to the throne, but instead he waited on God's perfect timing.

So we know we have to wait because that's just what is often necessary; this is what it takes to bear fruit and bear it well. But what I desperately want to know is this: is there anything under the sun I can do while I'm here waiting around for the fruit to show up? Can I at least fill up the watering can or shove a hose under the tree? *Anything?* Because if there isn't, I just might lose my mind. Can you identify with me here?

Today we are going to turn our attention to another man well acquainted with waiting; his name is Abraham. Let's jump in. Turn to Genesis 12 and read the first three verses.

In this very famous promise, God guarantees to Abraham some pretty incredible things. Make a list of what they are, here.

Here we find a promise similar to that of David's; of course, his is connected to a physical throne, and this one is a little more vague in nature, but the idea is the same. Abraham finds out he is going to be a big deal. A really big deal. At least, that's my summation of those three verses. "All peoples on earth will be blessed through you," God promises in Genesis 12:3. Now I can think of some fairly influential people: Mother Teresa and Gandhi immediately come to my mind. Or, more specific to our own country's history, there's Abraham Lincoln or Martin Luther King Jr. All accomplished great things that altered the lives of millions. But none could boast that every single person on earth benefited from or was blessed by their life's work. Abraham can. How? Write about it here.

Turn to Matthew 1:1 and complete this sentence.

This is the genealogy of Jesus the Messiah, the son of David, the _____ of Abraham (Matthew 1:1).

All people are blessed through Abraham because it's through his family line that Jesus is born. And Jesus changes everything. We are told in Ephesians 1 that "God has blessed us in the heavenly realms with every spiritual blessing *in Christ.*" What kind of blessing are we talking about here? One in which we are adopted to sonship (Eph. 1:4), redeemed and forgiven of our sins (Eph. 1:7), chosen (Eph. 1:11), and gifted with Holy Spirit (Eph. 1:13). These only come through Christ.

Let's imagine Abraham in this scene. God shows up and lays out this grand promise. A promise which, by the way, not only does Abraham not see in his lifetime or his children's lifetime, but one that is not fulfilled until thousands of years later. Now that is some waiting! Is there a promise like that in your life? One that seems unfathomable? One that feels so far beyond reach it's funny? One that you're positive will never come to fruition in your lifetime? If something comes to mind, please write it here.

Turn to Genesis 11:30. What does it say about Sarah?

Keep tracking with me here. God promises Abraham all people will be blessed through him, but there's a reality at work in this story that is sobering and makes the promise feel outright impossible: Sarah is barren. How can all people be blessed when not even one can be blessed through him?

Have you ever been waiting on God for an "I have to" and, when it finally comes, it seems so ridiculous and outside the realm of possibility that it's laughable. Write about this "I have to" below.

So what do we do with an "I have to," or a promise given to us by God that we know with certainty requires waiting? Abraham teaches us something about this as well. What does Genesis 12:4, 5 say he did?

Ever been in these times? When you're in a holding pattern, waiting for what has been promised? When you're yearning for that thing out there on the horizon, just beyond your vision, and still more obedience is required? And it's often obedience . . . *in spite of.* "OK, Abraham," God says. "I'm going to make you great, but here's what you have to do first; leave your father's house and go to a place that I will show you." This is an extraordinary request at any level, but it's made even more profound by the fact that Abraham is aging, his wife is barren, and he doesn't even know where he is going.[61] This is what I mean by "obedience in spite of." It doesn't always make a whole lot of sense to us, and it usually costs us something.

FOR ABRAHAM, IT BEGAN WITH ONE STEP TOWARD A LAND THAT WAS NOT HIS OWN. SO, LET ME ASK YOU: ON YOUR JOURNEY, WHAT STEP OF OBEDIENCE IS GOD CALLING YOU TO RIGHT NOW?

Abraham's story is the first time in Scripture our faith life is portrayed through the metaphor of a journey. Of course, it's a theme that will run steady through the remainder of the Old Testament and be picked up in and through the writings of many New Testament disciples. "The life of faith is one which keeps Israel in pursuit of the promise of land."[62] The end goal is to possess the land, but there will be many steps along the way, each one significant in their own right. And each step requires obedience from the sojourner.

When I felt compelled to write my first Bible study, it seemed like an extraordinarily daunting task. I had four kids; they were all under six years old. I had a husband in ministry, which, let's be honest, meant I was under obligation to give large amounts of time to the church. Don't read frustration into my words here; I did not give of my time grudgingly. I was honored to serve, and it fed me deeply. But finding time and energy for my "I have to" was challenging, to say the least.

But it started with one step, one prayer, one word, one sentence, one paragraph, one page. Over time, it became more. For Abraham, it began with one step toward a land that was not his own. So, let me ask you: on your journey, what step of obedience is God calling you to right now?

61 Bruce Feiler, *Abraham: A Journey to the Heart of Three Faiths* (New York: Harper Collins, 2004) p. 40.

62 Walter Brueggemann, *Genesis: Interpretation: A Bible Commentary for Teaching and Preaching* (Presbyterian Publishing Corporation). Kindle Edition.

It does not necessarily have to be something big. I say that because we often believe that it does. Maybe it's simply to turn the music off in the car and pray more often instead. Maybe it's to give one hour of your week to a local nonprofit located in an area you feel especially passionate about. Maybe it's to begin that book you always wanted to write or that workout program you said you would start yesterday. I don't know what that first step of obedience looks like for you. What I do know is, it is most likely going to feel uncomfortable at first. Leaving what we know for what is unknown is always going to involve fear on one level or another. I'm quite certain Abraham felt it as, with each passing step, he moved away from certainty and toward uncertainty. But it was worth it. Abraham is in the lineage of Jesus: talk about blessing, talk about it being worth it. The good news is, so are we.

First John 1:3 says, "See what great love the Father has lavished on us, that we should be called children of God! And that is what we are!"

What are we called?

If I'm not mistaken, being called His children inserts us directly into the center of the lineage too! When God gives us an "I have to," it's because, right around the corner, perhaps just out of sight, is a huge blessing. Partnering with God, as his beloved children, included in His plan and purposes, you will never know greater delight or joy. It's worth it. So worth it.

So let me revisit the question I posed earlier and give you real space to marinate on it. What step of obedience is God calling you to *right now*?

How can you reach for the unfathomable by doing the fathomable?

Day 4: The How Question
Genesis 14:1–7, 15:1–5

As we departed yesterday, I asked you an important question, and I hope the Lord has brought you an answer. If there is one specific step of obedience you have felt a particular pull toward, take a moment and write it again below.

Today we are going to continue on with the story of Abraham. When we left off, Abraham had taken that arduous, even painful first step of obedience. The one in which he left his father's household behind, ushering him toward a new and unknown land. Not just any land, but a land he was told would one day belong to his offspring.

So Abram—that was his name at the time, before God renamed him—with his large entourage, his wife Sarai, his nephew Lot, and all the possession he had acquired in his years at Harran, set out for this new land (Genesis 14:6). Just imagine packing up your entire household of stuff and loading it onto a whole bunch of camels and trekking it all through the desert. This is essentially what Abram did.

I can somewhat relate. And although I haven't had to drive a large moving van across the country with all of my possessions, many of you probably have. I *have* carted all four of my children along with the immense amount of *stuff* that they come with (even if it's only for a weeklong vacation) across the desert to a land flowing with milk and honey (or, in other words, a land with an ocean) called California. And yes, I drove all that way. OK, my husband drove all of that way, and in an air-conditioned car. (Quite shockingly, I know, we didn't use camels as our preferred mode of transportation.) But let me just tell you, even with no camels, that journey alone (hours in a car full of small children) was enough to put a few gray hairs on my head. I can only imagine what that was like for Abram, Sarai, and Lot.

Now, after sweat and tears, and probably some blood, they finally do arrive at this great and wonderful land that will belong to Abram and his future generations, but there's one little problem. Actually there are two minor—ahem, major—problems. Who is living in the land? (See Genesis 14:6.)

The Lord then appears to Abram and reinforces, one more time: "To *your* . . ." So, to whom will He give the land? (See Genesis 14:7.)

So this land, as great as it is, is actually inhibited by the Caananites and, at this point, there is still no offspring. So, if I'm Abram, I'm asking God: "Now, how is this all going to happen again? Because at this point, God, we've got two strikes against us." This question of *how*, my friends, is exactly what Abram asks. Read Genesis 15:1–4. Here, as you've noticed, we find a very interesting conversation that occurs between Abram and God. In order to get it straight in our heads, let's write it out as just that: a conversation.

> *God:*   *"Do not be _____, Abram.*
> *I am your _____,*
> *Your very great _____"* (Genesis 15:1).

> *Abram:*   *"Sovereign Lord, what can you _____*
> *_____ since I remain childless and the one who*
> *will inherit my estate is Eliezer of Damascus? You*
> *have given me no _____, so a servant of*
> *my household will be my heir"* (Genesis 15:2).

> *God:*   *"This man will not be your heir, but a son who is your*
> *own flesh and blood will be your heir. Look up at*
> *the sky and count the stars—indeed if you can count*
> *them. So shall your offspring be"* (Genesis 15:4, 5).

First, I love that God starts with, "Do not be afraid." Because He's acknowledging to Abram that fear is a very real and respectable state of emotion. When you've gone out on a limb, trusting in a God you barely know and walking away from what's comfortable to what is very uncomfortable, you're scared. And guess what? That's normal, and God affirms that. To add to this fear, there's no precedence for this kind of activity or dialogue between God and humanity—at least not any that Abram is aware of. Bruce Feiler writes, "Abraham, rooted in a polytheistic society—a world where gods had form and physicality and were identified with tangible facets of daily life, like rocks and tress—is prepared to put his trust in a-physical, indiscernible, unprovable god. Abraham is a visionary."[63] But even visionaries need small amounts of proof from time to time, and this is precisely what Abram is petitioning God for in the conversation we recorded above.

Abram could be saying these very words: "OK, God, I've heard your voice. You've told me about this great blessing, but now I'd really like to know how in the world you see this all coming together. I've got a perfectly good servant here. I mean, is that what you've got in mind, because I don't really see any other available opportunities at this point."

Abram lays it out here, doesn't he? He doesn't hold back or shy away from asking God the tough questions. "What can you give me?" he petitions God, point-blank (see Genesis 15:2).

---

63 Bruce Feiler, *Abraham: A Journey to the Heart of Three Faiths* (New York: Harper Collins, 2004) p. 41.

"Because if this whole thing is going to work out, I'm going to need a few more tangibles to go off of here." (He doesn't say these words exactly, but in my mind this is the sentiment being communicated.)

Have you ever felt that way? *OK, God, if I'm going to do what you're asking me to do here, I need something I can really sink my teeth into.* If so, elaborate about that particular time and circumstance.

This, for me, is one of the greatest, what I like to call, *"Phew!"* moments we experience in the Scriptures—at least in the Torah. The first one comes when Adam and Eve eat of the fruit of the tree of the knowledge of good and evil. You know, the exact one God explicitly told them not to touch. Their minds are opened, and not in a good way. They glance down and notice for the first time they are naked. Ashamed, alone, totally embarrassed, and now undeniably aware of their shortcomings, they try to hide from God. Which, by the way, never works. And what does God do? He sews them clothes! (See Genesis 3:21.) He meets them in the depth of their depravity with a peace offering called grace. And these are far more than clothes; they are proof that this God is a God of love. A truth John would record thousands of years later in one of his letters, a truth birthed in this moment in the garden. "Whoever does not love does not know God, because God is love" (1 John 4:8).

The second *Whew!* moment happens here within the story of Abram in Genesis 15. Abram, in essence, talks back to the teacher. He's the disgruntled employee complaining to his boss. And guess what? He doesn't get sent to the principal, and he doesn't get fired. We learn here that it's OK to question God. Honesty is not only allowed, it's actually preferred. Of course, there's an important distinction to make here. Abram wants to trust God; he just needs some help, a few metaphorical handles to grab onto. One commentary says: "To some degree, this question doubted God. Yet we can discern the difference between a doubt that *denies* God's promise and a doubt that *desires* God's promise. Abram *wanted* to believe and looked to God to strengthen his faith."[64]

This is very similar to the man in Mark we studied earlier in a different week of study. Remember his cry in response to Jesus? "I believe. Help my unbelief."

Something about that heartfelt longing for greater depths of faith honors God, even when there's an insufficiency of faith at work in the current moment. This gives me great hope.

---

64 David Guzik, *Verse by Verse Commentary on Genesis* (Santa Barbara, California: Enduring Word Media, 2012).

I can't say it any better than Walter Brueggemann: "The entire passage is one of a sharp exchange in which Abraham stands face to face with God and seeks to refute the promise and resist the assurance. Clearly, the faith to which Abraham is called is not a peaceful, pious acceptance. It is a hard-fought and deeply argued conviction. Abraham will not be a passive recipient of the promise. He is prepared to hold his own."[65]

Abram stands and questions, in "sharp dialogue" as we read above, and God actually . . . *responds*! Does he give him the full picture? No. Does he disclose every detail? No. It would still be *twenty-five years* from this exchange before Abram's blood son Isaac would be born to him and Sarai.[66] But God does respond. And He does so with the vision that was once "all peoples will blessed through you" (Genesis 12:3), a vision narrowed and specified to "a son who is your own flesh and blood will be your heir" (Genesis 15:4). Abram doesn't get all the answers, but he gets enough; he receives what he needs. And that is courage and resolve to take the next step forward in his journey.

Do you need this kind of response from God today? Are you, like Abram, asking the *how* question?

I wish I could guarantee that tonight, when you lay your weary head to rest, He would speak to you in a vision like He did with Abram. Of course, you already know I can't do that. But I hope this part of Abram's story allows you at least a temporary, or perhaps even more lasting, breath of relief. I hope it offers you a *Whew!* moment.

Let's rejoice in the fact that it's OK to say to God, "What can you give me?," just as Abram did.

And it's acceptable, or perhaps even more than just "acceptable," to admit to Him that, today, for whatever reason, your faith needs strengthening.

I believe this passage proves our God is a God of response. It's not a one-sided dialogue with Him. Our answers may come in an unexpected package, and they may not come immediately (remember, this is a chapter about waiting), but they will come.

Take the last few moments of today's lesson to write out your prayer. Be sure to begin with honesty, and don't shy away from your tough questions. I assure you, He can handle it.

---

65 Walter Brueggemann, *Genesis: Interpretation: A Bible Commentary for Teaching and Preaching* (Presbyterian Publishing Corporation). Kindle Edition 3313.

66 David Guzik, *Verse by Verse Commentary Genesis* (Santa Barbara, California: Enduring Word Media, 2012).

Day 5: Do You Believe?

We've been on a journey with Abram these last two days, and today is set up to be the climax to that story. As a reminder of where we left off yesterday, write out the question Abram confronts God with in Genesis 15:4.

Abram is not afraid to ask the tough questions. We learned from our previous lesson that God isn't afraid of them either. He provides reassurance to Abram that Eliezer of Damascus will not have to stand in as a firstborn son. God responds directly to Abram's queries by stating, "A son who is your own flesh and blood will be your heir."

Of course, at this point, all Abram has is a promise. There is still no son. Sarai is still not pregnant, and she won't be for twenty-five more years! There remains one more question that must be addressed, but this time not by God—by Abram.

It's a question none of us can avoid.

Do I believe?

"To be a descendant of Abraham is to live in the gap—to glance back to your native land, to peer ahead to your nameless destination, and to wonder, do I have the courage to make the leap?"[67]

Do I believe?

This is a question we each must answer for ourselves. The answer to that question for Abram can be found in Genesis 15:6. Read it and fill in the blanks below.

Abram _____ *the Lord, and he credited it to him as* ____ _____ *(Genesis 15:6).*

This is as confusing a phrase as I've come across in the Scriptures, and yet nearly every theologian would argue it's the basis for much of the gospel. So what does it mean? I need to know, not just for the sake of Abram, but for my own sake as well. To help us all decode this semi-foreign language, allow me to relate a story.

I have written a great deal so far in this study about my family's "I have to," the one that involved leaving our home church and launching into the unknown and terrifying land of church planting. As I write this day's study, we are nineteen days from our launch. We have the unique privilege of sharing space with another church within our denomination (or movement, as we refer to it). They have given us the gift of space to meet in rent free. This is every church planter's dream. Valley Community Church of

---

67 Bruce Feiler, *Abraham: A Journey to the Heart of Three Faiths* (New York: Harper Collins, 2004), pp. 43–44.

God has been around for more than fifty years. This incredibly sweet and charming church with a white steeple is tucked into a neighborhood called Arcadia. Arcadia is rapidly becoming one of the most trendy neighborhoods in greater Phoenix. It is filled with hip new restaurants and shops and populated with young professionals and young families who have been drawn to the neighborhood by its appeal.

If you were to walk inside this quaint church, you would find rows of pews, an organ, hymnals, and lecterns. Its 1960s character has been pristinely preserved and kept in nearly perfect condition. There are about fifty congregants, mostly in their seventies and eighties. So, like many of its era, this church is dying. Certainly not dying in its enthusiasm and vigor for the Lord, but for many in its community, time is literally running short. And yet, when my husband and I approached the pastor and his leadership team and asked about the possibility of sharing space, they welcomed us with open arms. Unlike many of their compatriots, who are willing to die defending their territory, they opened their doors and opened them wide. And we will forever be grateful for their generosity.

Of course, there were a few logistical hurdles to cross. Our kids—thirteen in our launch team alone—needed space to meet on Sunday evenings,

> PERHAPS YOU, LIKE ABRAM, ARE EXPERIENCING SOME KIND OF BARRENNESS, AND HOPELESSNESS SEEMS TO BE THE DEFINING CHARACTERISTIC OF THE STORY LINE OF THIS SEASON OF YOUR LIFE.

which meant some rearranging and spring cleaning on their part. And with that came another huge task. Our dream was to gather in the evenings, worship God, and then, directly following service, provide food and a place to gather and eat together as a church family. Knowing the number of people in our congregation could climb to nearly one hundred, we knew there was no space available for a gathering this large. So we met with the church board and pastor and asked, with baited breath, "Could we lay some cement out back, pouring over some of the existing grass field, to create an outdoor patio?" Can you see why I termed this a *big ask*? Of course, we assured them it would be done with the utmost professionalism. We told them we had a contractor as part of our team and promised he would ensure it was all done correctly. We were quite positive they would say no to this request. Who would trust a bunch of thirty-somethings they hardly knew with something like this? But to our shock and surprise, they agreed. They took us at our word. But more than that, they believed in us. And they said yes.

This, friends, is exactly what Abram does. He doesn't know God all that well yet. As we discussed yesterday, there is no precedent for this kind of God/humanity relationship.

But Abram decides to take him at His word, and even goes one step further. He *believes* Him. It's wonderful to trust the Word and promises of God, but when one key promise in your life isn't fulfilled for twenty-five years, how do you believe in spite of the facts? How do you trust, even when "wait" remains the defining discourse? This kind of belief can only exist because it rests firmly, not only in the words and promises of God, but even more so in His character.

The word used here for "believed" in the Hebrew is *aman*, and it's defined as "considering something to be trustworthy. . . . The meaning here is that Abram was full of trust and confidence in God and did not fear Him. It was not primarily in God's words that he believed, but in God himself."[68]

Can you remember a time you believed in someone, not because of what they said, but because of who they *are*? Or have you experienced someone believing in you this way? Describe this time below.

"He (Abram) doesn't believe in God, he believes God."[69] It's an ever-so-subtle difference in sentence structure, but it's a critical difference when it comes to our understanding of the kind of belief we must strive for. You see, Abram trusted God, took Him at His word, and believed Him, with no real or tangible proof whatsoever. And ultimately, this belief is what was credited to him as righteousness. "The text announces afresh what it means to be the human creatures we are created to be, that is, to be righteous. It means to trust God's future and to live assured of that future even in the deathly present."[70]

Paul does a great job summing up this concept in his letter to the church at Rome. Read Romans 4:4, 5 from *The Message* translation (below). Underline what stands out to you from this passage.

If you're a hard worker and do a good job, you deserve your pay; we don't call your wages a gift. But if you see that the job is too big for you, that it's something only God can do, and you trust him to do it—you could never do it for yourself no matter how hard and long you worked—well, that trusting-him-to-do-it is what gets you set right with God, by God. Sheer gift (Romans 4:4, 5, MSG).

68 James Strong, LLD, STD, *Strong's Expanded Exhaustive Concordance of the Bible* (Nashville: Thomas Nelson Publications, 2010), p. 539.

69 Bruce Feiler, *Abraham: A Journey to the Heart of Three Faiths* (New York: Harper Collins, 2004), p. 44.

70 Walter Brueggemann, *Genesis: Interpretation: A Bible Commentary for Teaching and Preaching* (Presbyterian Publishing Corporation). Kindle Edition.

How did Abram trust God with a "job too big" for him, one which he could never do himself?

I know as I write this, many of you find yourselves in all manner of difficult circumstances. Some of you have lost a loved one and are drowning in a sea of grief, and healing feels like a job far too great for you to handle. Some of you are new parents, and you feel underqualified and overwhelmed by the job of raising a child. Some of you have been let go from your job, handed a devastating diagnosis, or are witnessing the total unravelling of your marriage, perhaps experiencing the sting of a loved one's betrayal—these sorts of things go on and on. We are planting a church, which we are well aware requires strength and wisdom far beyond our thirty-two years. Perhaps you, like Abram, are experiencing some kind of barrenness, and hopelessness seems to be the defining characteristic of the story line of this season of your life.

Is this you? What job or task that lies ahead of you seems like something "only God" can do? Write about that here.

How can you believe God in the midst of your barrenness?

Is there a characteristic of God that you need to be reminded and reassured about? What is it?

As we close today, and this week of study, I've included a list of important characteristics and some Scriptures to go along with them. If one jumps out at you and resonates, take a few minutes to meditate on it. It might even help to grab a stickie note or even your phone and write it out. Keep it with you, memorize it, let it breathe life into your weary soul. Let's trust Him to do what only He can do. Let's be driven to greater places of obedience even when the outcome of that obedience remains unknown.

Peace

For he himself is our peace, *who has made the two groups one and has destroyed the barrier, the dividing wall of hostility* (Ephesians 2:14).

Love

But in all these things we overwhelmingly conquer through Him who loved us. *For I am convinced that neither death, nor life, nor angels, nor principalities, nor things present, nor things to come, nor powers, nor height, nor depth, nor any other created thing, will be able to separate us from the love of God, which is in Christ Jesus our Lord* (Romans 8:37-39).

Presence

"But the Advocate, the Holy Spirit, whom the Father will send in my name, will teach you all things and will remind you of everything I have said to you" (John 14:26).

Confidence

For the Spirit God gave us does not make us timid, but gives us power, love, and self-discipline (1 Timothy 1:7).

Hope

And not only this, but we also exult in our tribulations, knowing that tribulation brings about perseverance; and perseverance, proven character; and proven character, hope; and hope does not disappoint, because the love of God has been poured out within our hearts through the Holy Spirit who was given to us (Romans 5:4).

Power

I can do all this through him who gives me strength (Philippians 4:13).

THE NONSENSICAL "I HAVE TO"

This week, I'd like to switch the order of the review and Week Setup. **Let's review these questions from week four of our personal study.**

Day 1

1. What does the mere thought of waiting conjure up in you?

    How long was it between when David was anointed king and when he actually took the throne?

2. Review the sections of David's story we discussed in this day's lesson. Which of these situations would have been the most difficult for you to endure? Why?

3. What kinds of fruit was produced in David's life because of these challenging circumstances?

4. Has your "I have to" ever become an "I have to wait?"

Are you in a holding pattern now?

Day 2
1. What do the words *anoint* and *consecrate* mean in the original language?

2. What did Aaron have to wear when he entered the tabernacle?

3. What kind of clothing are we to wear (Colossians 3:12)? Are these characteristics built in us immediately or over time?

4. What kind of character is God building in you right now?

Day 3
1. What does God promise Abraham?

2. Have you ever been waiting on God for an "I have to," and when it finally comes, it seems so ridiculous and outside the realm of possibility that it's laughable?

3. Wherever you find yourself in your faith journey, what step of obedience is God calling you to *right now*?

Day 4

1. When they arrive, who is living in the land that God promised to Abram and his descendants?

2. Have you ever felt like Abram, longing to trust the promise of God but needing a bit more to go on? If so, elaborate here.

3. What do you need from God to take further steps of faith with the "I have to" that's been assigned to you? This story is proof you can ask Him for what you need. We too can say to God, as Abram did, "What can you give me?" What is your response to that knowledge?

Day 5

1. Can you remember a time when you believed in someone, not because of what they said but because of who they are? Have you experienced someone believing in you this way? Write about either, or both.

2. What stands out to you from Romans 4:4, 5 and why?

3. What job or task that lies ahead of you seems like something only God can do? Why?

4. How can you believe God in the middle of barrenness in your life?

Watch Session 5 at Christyfay.com: When "I have to" means "I have to wait"

The Setup

In March 2014 I reached a tipping point. I couldn't ignore it any longer: there was a nagging and tugging at my soul that literally refused to be ignored. I laid my daughter down for her afternoon nap, threw on a TV show for my son's "quiet time," and then pressed "print" on my computer. With the printer talking in the background, I watched page after page emerge: chapters of Scripture, countless verses, and blank spaces. What would God say and what inspiration would He implant in my Spirit?

I wasn't sure. I wouldn't have called it this at the time, but what I had on my hands was an "I have to." I was to write a Bible study. The mandate came with both a weight and a clarity unmatched by anything I'd experienced to that point in my life. The stories of five distinct and unique women found in the lineage of God's Son was the topic. A quiet but convincing voice urged me forward: "Don't think. Just start. Ready, set, go."

Over the course of the year-plus it took me to write that study, I wrestled with the kinds of questions you might expect. *Did I have any idea what I was doing? Who in the world was going to read this? Wasn't I grossly underqualified for such a task? Was I crazy?* This whole "God's calling you to write a Bible study" thing—had I made it all up in my head? Was I a mad person slaving away over my computer in my home office, day after day, with no real clue if any of it would mean anything to anyone, ever?

Have you ever had this kind of experience, one in which you feel compelled—called—to something that doesn't necessarily make a lot of sense? Have you ever wondered if you've temporarily, or perhaps more permanently, lost your mind?

The truth is, our "I have to's" frequently can make us feel this way—like mad people, that is.

Take, for example, Galileo, who was quite convinced that, contrary to popular thought, it was not the Earth that sat at the center of the solar system, but the Sun. Ridiculed, scoffed at, and labeled as a fool, he was forbidden to teach any such theories and later sentenced to life imprisonment; lucky for him, it was later reduced to house arrest.[71] His "I have to" certainly seemed, to most observers, completely nonsensical.

The Wright brothers, of Dayton, Ohio, credited as the first individuals to ever fly a mechanized airplane heavier than air and under its own power, had a similar experience as Galileo.

"Along with the costs of experiments in flight, the risk of humiliating failure, injury, and, of course, death, there was the inevitable prospect of being mocked as a crank, a crackpot, and in many cases for good reason . . . long before the Wright brothers took

---

71 "Galileo Galilei," BBC News / BBC History, bbc.co.uk, © 2015, BBC. Accessed March 1, 2016.

up their part, would-be 'conquerors of the air' and their strange and childish flying machines, as described in the press, had served as a continuous source of comic relief."[72] One newspaper asserted: "Man can't fly."[73] Of course, the Wrights would continue, in spite of opposition and all types of challenges, to believe flight was well within the realm of possibility. And in Le Mans, France just eight years into the twentieth century (and five years after their first actual flight in December 1903 in North Carolina), they proved—this time with the entire world watching—that they were right.[74]

The stories of these three men teach us that there will always be those who stand in disapproval, convinced that our "I have to" is ludicrous and altogether unattainable. And sometimes, as was the case for King David, those closest to us throw the first and most painful stone. When it was time to move the ark of the covenant to its home and resting place in Jerusalem, David accompanied it. Along with the other priests, David worshipped and danced, rejoicing in the significance of a monumental event. Wearing a linen ephod (the appropriate attire of a priest), the text tells us, "David was dancing before the Lord with all of his might" (2 Samuel 6:14). There is one onlooker, however, who was far from impressed by David's unashamed worship and celebration before the Lord. His own wife, Michal, watched from a nearby window, and his performance caused her so much distress and embarrassment that she despised David in her heart. She goes on to scold him brashly: "How the king of Israel has distinguished himself today, going around half-naked in full view of the slave girls of his servants as any vulgar fellow would!" (2 Samuel 6:20)

> **DAVID IS SAYING: YOU MIGHT CALL ME CRAZY, BUT I'LL TAKE EVERY CRITICISM YOU CAN HURL, AND I'LL STAND MY GROUND.**

A question: What if these men hadn't pushed through in spite of the criticism? What if they had succumbed to others' expectations of them instead of striving for a dream yet unproven? What if they had stayed where it was safe and comfortable instead of finding the courage to conquer unchartered territory? Our world would be very different today if not for the unparalleled risks of men and women like the ones I've described here.

Our "I have to's" will inevitably feel nonsensical; history serves as undeniable proof of that fact. One question remains: What will we do in the face of criticism, mocking, and outright persecution? How will we react when others point, laugh, snicker, and say,

72 David McCulllough, *The Wright Brothers* (New York: Simon and Schuster, 2015), p. 33.

73 Ibid.

74 Ibid, p. 173.

"That (whatever your *that* is) doesn't make any sense"? David gives us insight with his response to Michal: "I will celebrate before the Lord. I will become even more undignified than this, and I will be humiliated in my own eyes" (2 Samuel 6:21, 22).

David is saying, You might call me crazy, but I'll take every criticism you can hurl, and I'll stand my ground. This is my "I have to," and I will lay down my ego, sacrifice my reputation, and risk it all because of the One who gave me the assignment.

This week we examine what happens when your "I have to" is nonsensical. My hope for us all is that, at the end of our five days of study, we take a page from David's book and learn to dance unashamedly in spite of who's watching.

THE NONSENSICAL "I HAVE TO"

Day 1: "Because You Say So . . . "
Luke 5:1–7

Today we begin with a story about Peter. When we first meet him, he'll be called Simon, but Peter is the name that will make the history books. I really like Peter; I mean, I *really* like him. He's passionate and committed one moment and, the next, wavering and uncertain. He is loyal and overexuberant, but with the flip of the switch he quickly dissolves into lackluster, unconvinced. I like him because he's real. His near-schizophrenic behavior makes me feel as though my own irrational tendencies are seminormal. We need Peters in our lives; they remind us that it's OK to be the best version of ourselves one day and the absolute worst version of ourselves the next. The best news is these are precisely the kinds of people Jesus targets in the recruitment phase of his ministry. Could-be saints, those who just need a few nudges here and there to be reminded of what they are capable of.

Read Luke 5:1–7 and then answer a few basic questions to get started.

What is Simon's (Peter's) profession?

What is Jesus' profession? (See Matthew 13:55.)

What is Peter's response when Jesus tells him to put out into deep water and let down the nets for a catch?

Let's pretend for a brief moment that you are a surgeon. A very successful neurosurgeon. (As an aside, if you're going to daydream, it's nice to imagine yourself in roles such as these, the kinds in which the lives of those around you lie in your talented and capable hands.) OK! Back to the question at hand. What would you do if the CEO of a food distribution company walked into your operating room and started telling you how to do your job?

I'm going to go out on a limb here and assume you would feel angry, irritated, and more than just a bit frustrated. You might call security and ask for this person to be quietly and calmly escorted out of your operating room and, furthermore, directly from the hospital. This is how Peter might have felt! Jesus is a carpenter, as you now know, and Peter a fisherman. Last time I checked, these two professions had little if anything to do with each other. And yet, in this moment, Jesus asserts that he is more than qualified to send Peter and his companions back out to sea after a dull and unsuccessful night of fishing. Which, by the way, goes against the number one rule fishermen not only obey but structure their livelihood around. "The fish are more likely to be caught after dark. On this occasion the men had worked all night for nothing; the last thing they would normally do would be to start again by daylight."[75] Rule number one: you fish at night.

We're calling this week "The Nonsensical 'I Have To.'" And friends, Jesus asking Peter to "put out into deep water and let down the nets for a catch" (vs. 4) is utterly nonsensical. Oh, and by the way, they've just met. Jesus decides to use Peter's boat as his speaking platform—literally, his speaking platform—and then, as an aside, He turns to him and says, "Yeah, I think it's time to fish again." How's that for first impressions? I have the sense that, as I write, some of you might be new to this whole God-Jesus-faith thing. If you are, then you're just like Peter in this story! And as it was for Peter so it is for you; Jesus very well might ask you to do something that feels—well, crazy—for lack of a better way of saying it. Perhaps the thought of putting your trust in God has you feeling a little unhinged. If that's you, I get it. Having faith in the unseen and intangible is not the most logical thing to do. But we'll see from this story that it certainly has its payoffs. For you, the "deep water" you're compelled to navigate toward might simply be

---

75 Tom Wright, *Luke for Everyone (New Testament for Everyone)*, SPCK. Kindle Edition, p. 54.

belief in general. But for all of us, no matter where we find ourselves on our faith journey, there's always deep water. What place is God calling you toward that seems downright nonsensical?

I wish I was super handy, that I could fix things around the house. You know, like rewire a light fixture or hang a really heavy shelf without fear that my poor installation will result in an emergency room trip with one of my kids. But the bottom line is that I can't do these things. Every once in a while I think I can. So I set about the task of installing a new door handle or hanging a fan or whatever. I work really hard, I sweat, I usually curse, and I read and reread the instructions, but they might as well be in Chinese. After all that, I usually call my mom. She is Martha Stewart without the cooking inclinations, and a little bit of Chip Gaines thrown in. In her house, she owns the power tools, and they are pink. She's legit too; the girl knows how to handle a table saw. So, she's the first person I call when I give in and give up, after I've thrown in the towel because I've nearly electrocuted myself or sawed off one of my fingers.

Point is, this is where Peter finds himself. He's worked hard all night and hasn't caught one measly fish. Of course, the clear difference between him and me is that he's actually an expert fisherman and I'm just a wannabe handy woman. When we get to the end of our ropes, when what we've tried just isn't working, we're forced to ask for help, or at least entertain the idea of it.

Have you ever felt like Peter? Perhaps you've worked really hard at something and, in the end, in spite of your best efforts, it just wasn't enough. You came up short.

Ultimately, this is what leads Peter to what he says next. Fill in the blanks from Luke 5:5.

"Master, we've worked hard all night and haven't caught anything. But _____ _____ _____ _____, I will let down the nets."

At this point, I'm positive that Peter is far from convinced that Jesus' way is better than his. But he's also got to be thinking: I have nothing to show for a hard night's work, so why not? What's it going to hurt to just give it a shot?

Are you feeling a bit like Peter? Maybe a little more than skeptical about this off-the-wall "I have to" that's been thrust before you?

If so, you might need to have your "because you say so" moment with God.

So stop for a moment. Press the pause button on this day's study right now and ask God, "What do I need to say yes to even though it doesn't make sense?" Or, "What do I need to say no to even though it doesn't make sense?"

Did you ask Him? OK, good.

Now, finish the following sentence:

Because you say so I will . . .

We ended last week talking about obedience, and we've begun this week talking about obedience. Why? It's really the only right response. It's just that simple. And also that painfully difficult. And let me just point out: You can say *no*. I'm not going to judge you, and God is not going to force you into anything. However, if you say no there's a distinct possibility you might miss out on something pretty incredible. What would Peter have missed out on had he ignored Jesus? Read Luke 5:6, 7.

> SOMETIMES, WHEN WE SAY YES, OUR SPIRITUAL BOATS GET JAM-PACKED FULL OF FISH.

Sometimes, when we say *yes*, our spiritual boats get jam-packed full of fish. Sometimes, when we're obedient, we get to see the payoff instantly or at least within that week, month, or year. And sometimes it takes a really, really, *really* long time for our obedience to even make a dent. (We'll look at that scenario tomorrow.) For now, let me leave you with one question, and then a prayer.

What are you willing to say yes or no to, even though, in your right mind, you can't make sense of it? Write about it here.

Father, as we close today, may you give us all courage to, like Peter, proclaim, "Because you say so." Obedience is difficult and often costly, and yet waiting just behind the corner very well may be a blessing we will never receive unless we proceed in faith. We need your strength, your peace, and your power, for without it we have no hope. We love you. Amen.

Day 2: In It for the Long Haul
Genesis 6:9-22

My first ever true job in vocational ministry (I'm speaking about the one I actually got paid for) was as a children's pastor. During the time that I was on staff, the church transitioned from meeting in a high school auditorium to, for the first time in thirteen years, meeting in a building we could call our own. Part of my job entailed equipping and outfitting the new children's space. This was a fun but equally daunting task, especially because having just taken on the debt of a new church building, the budget for my project was—how can I say it?—on a shoestring. One of our preschool classrooms was called Noah's Kids. My very gracious cousin-in-love agreed to paint a mural of Noah, the ark, and a small collection of animals on the wall. She did a stunning job, and the kids loved it. The room has since been redecorated and the mural painted over, but I have a clear vision in my head of its original design. Sweet little old Noah cautiously and carefully ushering his rather varied array of elephants, tigers, zebras, and lions into the quaintly built ark— what would become their home for the next forty days and nights.

The story has been somewhat glorified over the years, and when I say "somewhat," I actually mean it's been grossly misrepresented. With that in mind, I'm going to ask you to read through this story with fresh eyes and, perhaps more importantly, a realistic perspective on the events that unfolded.

Read Genesis 6:9–22.

It's a strange story in more ways than one. The days in which Noah and his family lived were dark ones. The earth was polluted with all kinds of violence and corruption, the kind that would grieve the Creator's heart so deeply and trouble him so completely that the only solution was total destruction. But there existed one man, who was "righteous" and "blameless" (Genesis 6:9), and God would use this man and his family to set the course of human history straight. (We will talk at more length about this particular topic on a subsequent day of study.) For now, we are going to focus on exactly what God asked Noah to do. Let's outline the specific instructions given to our main character in regard to the construction of the ark.

What was it to be made of?

What did the rooms need to be coated with?

What were the dimensions of the ark?

How many decks were there to be?

Now, because we don't generally measure things in cubits anymore, let's take some time to outline the ark's dimensions using currents measurements. "The ark was as long as a 30-story building is high (about 450 feet or 150 meters), and it was about 75 feet (25 meters) wide and 45 feet (15 meters) high. What is described is not really a boat, but a well-ventilated barge, meant only to float and not to sail anywhere. After all, an *ark* is a chest, not a ship; this refers to the "shoebox" shape of the vessel."[76]

So what we are talking about here is a mammoth-sized, shoebox-shaped, boat-like object that was roughly the size of the *Titanic*! The *Titanic!* Can you even believe it? It wasn't until 1858 *A.D.* that a boat was constructed that was larger than this ark built by Noah.[77] We are talking thousands and thousands and thousands of years before anything of this nature is even dreamed of as possible. And then there's Noah, building this gigantic wood monstrosity. Think of the strange looks, the scowls, the jeers, the outright embarrassment he would have endured. Noah has hammer and nails in hand, working feverishly on his pet project, when a neighbor strolls by. The conversation goes something like this.

Neighbor: "Hey, Noah, what are you building?"

Noah: "Oh, just something to keep my family safe from the floodwaters when they come."

Neighbor: (*Laughing hysterically*) "Floodwaters, what do you mean 'floodwaters'? The only water I've ever heard of is oceans, seas, rivers, and streams. You mean to tell me water is just going to fall from the sky? If that's not the funniest thing I've ever heard, I don't know what is!"

---

76 David Guzik, *Verse by Verse Commentary Genesis* (Santa Barbara, California: Enduring Word Media, 2012).
77 Ibid.

(Calls out to his buddy and neighbor:)

"Hey, Dan, Noah thinks water is just going to up and fall from the sky! Maybe we should throw him in the barn with old man Abner. Nothing like a loony to keep another loony company!"

(He's now laughing so hard he can barely breathe.)

You think I'm making this all up? It is believed that at this time in human history rain didn't exist.[78] So to every onlooker Noah just looks and talks like a total and complete crazy person. I love how Eugene Peterson recounts this story in the faith chapter of Hebrews in the Message version: "By faith, Noah built a ship in the middle of dry land" (Hebrew 11:7, *MSG*). That phrase, by itself, is oxymoronic. Building a ship in the middle of dry land, with no large body of water in sight and no record of rain? Speaking of a nonsensical "I have to," I am convinced that there is none greater than the one mandated by God for Noah. So if your "I have to" is edging its way toward crazy, I hope you can at least now say, "I am not alone. Me and Noah are in the same boat." (And no pun is intended!)

If you can even believe it, there is one more aspect of this story that we have yet to discuss, one that throws the level of crazy all the way over the top: the length of time it would have taken to complete a floating structure of this magnitude, *by hand* no less.

There is no right or wrong answer here, but I'd love to know how long you guesstimate it would have taken Noah to build this ark? (Go ahead, wager a guess.)

I wish I had the exact answer, but the Scriptures don't reveal a specific timeline from start to finish. We do know it took 15,000 workers a little more than two years (1909–1911) to construct the *Titanic*.[79] I'm pretty sure Noah didn't have a whole lot of help other than from his family, and I'm assuming there weren't a whole lot of technological advances that sped the process along. The moral of the story is this: it would have taken a long time, a *long, long* time, to build this boat.

In yesterday's story Peter's "I have to" (letting the nets down for a catch) requires obedience. Lucky for him, his obedience produced clear and tangible results. The boat was so full of fish the fishermen had to call for more help. I'm not discounting that his was, in fact, a nonsensical "I have to." All I'm saying is, he got to see the payoff for his seemingly crazy act almost immediately. This couldn't be further from the truth for our friend Noah. Years passed before the rain that God spoke of actually came. In the meantime, he was left as the laughingstock of his entire region.

---

78 Ibid.

79 "How Big Was the Titanic?" http://www.titanicuniverse.com/how-big-was-the-titanic/1276 © 2013 Titanic Universe. Accessed March 21, 2016.

Have you been there? Are you there now? Has God called you to something that feels crazy? You too feel like the laughingstock of your family or group of friends? Share about those feelings here.

When we experience a nonsensical "I have to," sometimes our obedience yields results immediately, as with Peter. But sometimes it feels like we are in the trenches day after day. When we attempt to get out, more attacks come our way, bullets so close that they graze us and do just enough damage to force us to continue the battle, wounded. Sometimes it takes years—and lots of them—to see the fruit of our obedience. If you're feeling beat up right now, perhaps similar to how Noah must have felt, I want to invite you to close this day of study by meditating on some promises from God's Word. There is no sugarcoating it. It was not easy for Noah. Building a ship nearly as large as the *Titanic* on dry land, operating in a world in which rain was unheard of, and then herding two of every kind of living creature, along with their daily food intake, onto this massive barge. Who can fathom it? And

I LOVE HOW EUGENE PETERSON RECOUNTS THIS STORY IN THE FAITH CHAPTER OF HEBREWS IN THE MESSAGE VERSION: "BY FAITH, NOAH BUILT A SHIP IN THE MIDDLE OF DRY LAND" (HEBREW 11:7, *MSG*).

we haven't even talked of the amount of excrement Noah and his family would have had to deal with on a daily basis. Perhaps your nonsensical "I have to" feels this kind of crazy, on top of the fact that you are pretty sure it might take you half your life to find the rainbow at the end of it all (metaphorically speaking). It sure isn't easy for you either.

You will need to cling to these promises when persecution and trouble come. It can sometimes be tempting to hurry up and finish when you're so close to the end of a day of study. Do your best to read through these Scriptures carefully, slowly. What sticks out to you? If a word or a phrase jumps off the page, then circle it or underline it. If you feel God is using this verse to speak specifically into your circumstances, make a note of what He is saying in the margin. I'm praying for you, dear friends. Push through; there's a rainbow at the end. I can feel it.

But you will not leave in haste or go in flight; for the LORD will go before you, the God of Israel will be your rear guard (Isaiah 52:12).

In all your ways submit to him, and he will make your paths straight (Proverbs 3:6).

He will be the sure foundation for your times, a rich store of salvation and wisdom and knowledge; the fear of the LORD is the key to this treasure (Isaiah 33:6).

Cast all your anxiety on him because he cares for you (1 Peter 5:7).

You enlarge my steps under me, and my feet have not slipped (Psalm 18:36, NASB).

Being confident of this, that He who began a good work in you will carry it on to completion (Philippians 1:6).

Day 3: Chipping Away
Joshua 6:1–7

One of my kids' favorite summer activities is called Ice Treasures. This requires the parents—or a grandparent, which is mostly the case with us!—to freeze a whole bunch of dollar store items in a gigantic block of ice. The kids then get spoons and a myriad of other utensils to begin chipping away until they arrive at some kind of treasure embedded within the ice. All four of my kids get into this game, from my two-year-old to my eight-year-old. At some point along the way my younger kids usually get sidetracked, or just plain old tuckered out from all that hard work, and guess who's left in charge? If you said Grandma or Mom, you are correct. Let me be real with you: it's seriously hard labor to get those items free from their ice prison. Ice chips flying and barely dodging my eyeballs, my hand cramped from gripping the spoon, breathless, I shout for joy when I've extracted the last item.

It's a funny visual, I realize, but this is how it feels sometimes with our "I have to's." Ice pick in hand, we chip away, wondering if we're making any ground, dodging all kinds of metaphorical ice chips, flat-out exhausted. We're forced to wrestle with one question: I know other people think I'm crazy. Is it possible I am?

What do we do when we find ourselves in this position? Do we fight back against the feelings of doubt, or do we flee in the face of discouragement? Many of us don't intend to run out and slam the door on our nonsensical "I have to," but we simply don't possess the correct tools necessary to hunker down and stand strong. Today we are going to uncover a tool, and I would venture to say it's the most important one we'll need to fight the good fight.

Let's read Joshua 6:1–7. Answer these questions.

1. How many times are the Israelites to march around the city? How many days?

2. Seven priests are to carry trumpets of ram's horns in front of the what?

3. We talked about the ark of the Lord in a previous lesson; reference back to remind yourself of its purpose and significance. Write your findings here.

In this section of the story the commander of the army of the Lord (Joshua 5:15) is giving Joshua a military plan of attack. Of course, it's possible it's the worst one ever drafted. The armed men march behind a group of priests never before allowed into battle. It seems this plan should fail before it even begins. And if they were going for a surprise attack, well, let's just say it's hard to miss a group of men marching and a squadron of priests blowing horns. This model of warfare—then, and now—makes absolutely no sense. The "I have to" Joshua has been given certainly falls under the category of nonsensical. Of course, if this battle is going to be won, it will be won God's way.

Why do you think the commander of the Lord's army tells Joshua to take the ark of the covenant with priests and warriors?

Exactly! If they are going to win, it will not be in their own strength. It will not be because of their advanced weaponry, and it certainly won't be because of their cunning military intelligence. They will win purely and simply because God wants them to. And the ark will play a vital and crucial role in this victory. "Israel had to keep their hearts and minds on the LORD who was present with them, instead of putting their hearts and minds on the difficulty of the task in front of them."[80]

This is precisely what we *must* do if we are to succeed in the face of our challenging and nonsensical "I have to's." Our hearts must dwell not on how hard the task is, how crazy it seems, how long it might take, what results we do or do not see from our obedience— but on God, whose presence with us alone will sustain us.

I'd like to take a moment to revisit our friend Peter from our first day of study for this week. If you remember I wrote about how much I like him. Cold one minute and hot the next, Peter always gets so close to the hidden truth of who Jesus is and what He has called Peter to do—close and yet still so far. I feel that too, more often than I'd like to admit. Turn to Matthew 14:22-33 and answer these questions.

1. The disciples are on a boat at sea and Jesus has just finished praying on land nearby. How does Jesus get to them?

---

80 David Guzik, *Verse by Verse Commentary Joshua* (Santa Barbara, California: Enduring Word Media, 2012).

2. When Peter recognizes it's Jesus, what does he do?

3. What causes Peter to sink?

I've done this exact thing that Peter did. OK, no, clearly I have not walked on water. But I too have been filled with the adrenaline and excitement that comes from a nonsensical "I have to." I rush to the edge of the boat, pull my feet over the edge, and in a moment of bravery and courage I put my feet down. "Look everyone, I'm doing it!" I shout. But then reality slaps me in the face and not mere moments later I'm struck with the realization that there is wind and waves and a ton of other reasons to not be doing what I'm doing. Before I know it, I've plunged into the icy waters of doubt and discouragement. Can you relate?

Notice, of course, that when Peter's eyes lock on those of Jesus, he stays perfectly afloat. And yet, when just for a moment Peter's gaze is distracted by the winds and waves, the once-possible becomes impossible. Yes, before you say it, I will. (It might seem like a cliché, but remember, clichés only exist because they are true.) The only way to "walk on water" is to fix our eyes on Jesus. N.T. Wright wrote this.

> **I'M STRUCK WITH THE REALIZATION THAT THERE IS WIND AND WAVES AND A TON OF OTHER REASONS TO NOT BE DOING WHAT I'M DOING. BEFORE I KNOW IT, I'VE PLUNGED INTO THE ICY WATERS OF DOUBT AND DISCOURAGEMENT. CAN YOU RELATE?**

> What we are called to do—it's so basic and obvious, but so hard to do in practice—is to keep our eyes fixed on Jesus, and our ears open for his encouragement (even if it does contain some rebuke as well). And our wills and hearts must be ready to do what he says, even if it seems crazy at the time.[81]

81 N.T. Wright, *Matthew for Everyone, Part 1: Chapters 1–15* (New Testament for Everyone) (Westminster John Knox Press). Kindle Edition, p. 191.

The author of Hebrews would pen these words:

*Therefore, since we are surrounded by such a great cloud of witnesses, let us throw off everything that hinders and the sin that so easily entangles. And let us run with perseverance the race marked out for us, **fixing our eyes on Jesus**, the pioneer and perfecter of faith. For the joy set before him he endured the cross, scorning its shame, and sat down at the right hand of the throne of God. Consider him who endured such opposition from sinners, so that you will not grow weary and lose heart* (Hebrews 12:1-3, emphasis added).

Before we close today, please reflect on these questions.

1. Why is fixing our eyes on Jesus so simple in theory and yet so difficult in practice?

2. What are some practical steps you can take to "fix your eyes on Jesus"?

3. How can you let the encouragement and love of God quiet and displace your doubt and discouragement?

One final thought: at the end of the story of Peter's attempt to walk on water, we find the outstretched hand of Jesus. Just before Peter goes under, he is yanked to the surface. Jesus is there to catch him. Our failures are never the end of the story. God's saving grace always is. Do not feel shame or guilt for going under; those emotions only serve to drum up greater amounts of discouragement and doubt. Instead, hold tight to the outstretched hand of Jesus. Tomorrow is another day. Tomorrow is the day you just might walk on water.

Day 4: But Seriously: Why?
Judges 6:1–6, 15; 7:1–25

So far this week we've met Peter, a fisherman by trade, who encounters Jesus and, in doing so, is forced to confront his own nonsensical "I have to." We've come to understand how undeniably nonsensical Noah's "I have to" was and, in doing so, realized that our obedience does not always produce fast or immediate results. We've asked how, in light of these truths, we can persevere in the face of persecution, doubt, and discouragement. But there is one question that remains, and I bet it's been circling around in your heads these last few days as much as it has mine: *Why?* Why in the world does God choose to work this way? And by now you must have sensed a pattern emerging. There are very few characters in the Holy Scriptures that confront an "I have to" that is not at least remotely nonsensical—and usually it's flat-out crazy. In fact, we could extend this chapter by days and days and still not even come close to running out of stories from the Bible with the same type of narrative. God continually calls us to do things that seem, to outsiders, and sometimes even to ourselves, utterly crazy. From the hardest places of our own nonsensical "I have to's," we cry out to God: "Could you not have made this just a little easier, just a little less insane?" Have you ever asked that in your own faith journey? Can you recall a time? If so, write about it here.

So, the question is: *Why?* We can find keys to the answer in the story of a man named Gideon. For just a bit of background on him, turn to Judges 6:15. How does Gideon describe himself in this verse?

Not exactly a stellar resume, especially considering the task at hand. To get a sense of just how difficult a battle it would be for Gideon, we should understand the depth of evil inhabited by the Midianites. Take a moment to read Judges 6:1–6 and answer these questions.

1. How long were the Israelites oppressed by the Midianites?

2. Where were the Israelites forced to make their homes?

3. What happened to the Israelites and their land when the Midianites invaded?

Once again, here is the setup. Gideon, not a man known for courage, bravery, or strength—in fact, far from it—is hand-selected by God to lead the Israelites in a revolt against the Midianites. A people powerful, ruthless, and heartless who have savagely oppressed the Israelites for the last seven years. Once again, we are confronted with yet another nonsensical "I have to." And if you thought this part of the story seems crazy, just wait. Read what happens in Judges 7:1–3. Circle the correct answers below.

1. How many men do the Israelites begin with?

    32,000   50,000   100,000

2. How many men remain after the first test?

    12,000   10,000   5,000

Now read Judges 7:4–8.

3. After the second test, how many Israelite men remain?

    1,000   500   300

I warned you the story was about to get crazier! Gideon "had started the day with 32,000 men at his back. Now there are 300—a reduction of over 99 percent!"[82] At this point the Israelites have about the same chances of winning this battle as I do of getting drafted in the NFL by the Arizona Cardinals! Let's just say *none*.

What is God thinking? And perhaps more to the point of today's lesson, why does he have Gideon thin the troops down to such a minuscule number? The answer lies in the text we already read. Write out Judges 7:2 here; doing so will help it get deeper into your heart.

---

82 Timothy Keller, *Judges For You (God's Word For You)* (The Good Book Company). Kindle Edition.

I wish I wasn't prone to take the credit, steal the spotlight, and exalt myself when God alone deserves the glory, but I am. I wish I didn't care what other people thought so I didn't have to strive so hard to earn their approval, but I do. I wish I didn't believe my value and worth derives from how well I perform and what I produce, but that just isn't so. The truth is, if I'm not forced into the impossible, I'll stay in my comfort zone, where I get to call the shots on how my life gets lived. And if I'm not handcuffed to God by being stripped of my own agenda, I'll never learn to trust Him to do what only He can do. As humans we tend not to drift toward the exaltation of God; we are much more likely to drift toward the exaltation of ourselves. God knows this, and so, for our own best interest, He presses us into nonsensical "I have to's." It was true for Gideon and the Israelites, and it's still resoundingly true for us today.

> AS HUMANS WE TEND NOT TO DRIFT TOWARD THE EXALTATION OF GOD; WE ARE MUCH MORE LIKELY TO DRIFT TOWARD THE EXALTATION OF OURSELVES.

Timothy Keller wrote, "As soon as we begin to believe that we deserve credit for rescuing or delivering ourselves, we take away glory from God that he deserves. We set up ourselves as alternative saviors. This is the greatest spiritual danger there is—that we should believe that we can save, or have saved, ourselves."[83]

Have you ever believed you could save yourself? If so, where did it get you?

83 Keller, *Judges For You.*

In your own circumstances right now, can you see why God might be pushing you outside your comfort zone so you will learn to trust Him more? Journal about that here.

Before we close today I'd like you to take a few moments and finish the story. Read Judges 7:9–25.

Only God could win a battle with three hundred men and a bad dream. *Only God.* When I think about my life and how I hope others will remember it, my deepest desire is that others would reflect and say: "*Only God.*" She lived an incredible story, each chapter filled with such profound adventure that the only possible mastermind behind it all could be God. Unfortunately, adventure comes with a cost: It's called surrender. Surrender looks like saying yes in spite of a million reasons to say no. Surrender looks impossible to the eye and says, "Impossible? Nothing is impossible with God." Surrender lays down my right to govern and puts control in the hands of God.

May we all look back at the circumstances of our lives and say, "This victory was God's, not mine. My only part was to trust and obey him. The glory is his, and the privilege is mine."[84] And what a great privilege it is!

84 Keller.

Day 5: What's at Stake?
Scriptures below; several study texts on Noah and Peter

Jack was a senior pastor of a larger-sized congregation. Since he had stepped into the role, the church had grown significantly. The staff of the church seemed to work well together, the ministries were thriving, and Jack had the support of his board. Overall, there were very few hiccups.

Until one day when he was driving out to a neighboring city to play golf and he felt God place an "I have to" in his heart. This community was rapidly growing, and there were few churches he could spot. As time passed, it became hard to shake that strange stirring that had surfaced in the car that day. Eventually, Jack knew what he had to do. He would leave his comfortable position in an established church to begin a new community. His "I have to" seemed crazy, and many questioned him. But he knew in his spirit he had heard the voice of the Lord, and the only thing left to do was respond.

Sally was driving to church one morning. She was part of a vibrant community where she knew others and others knew her. She always looked forward to the weekly gatherings, and this morning was no different. But as she drove past another church building, one she had hardly noticed until this moment, she felt God whisper: *Turn.* "Now?" she questioned, every so quietly. *Here,* the voice firmly told her. And so she found herself among unfamiliar faces in an unfamiliar setting. A young woman had come to preach. Sally heard the woman say in her introduction that she wasn't the usual pastor or a member of the teaching team. Sally listened and, as the sermon came to an end, she felt compelled to go forward. Sally knew she needed to speak some words of encouragement, which she did. Then, seemingly out of nowhere, a somewhat strange question popped into Sally's head and she sure she needed to ask it: "Are you writing anything right now?" The preacher girl's eyes lit up. "Why yes. In fact I just finished the rough draft of my very first Bible study."

In these two stories both characters said yes to an "I have to" that didn't seem to make a whole lot of sense. And yet, without the obedience of these two people (I have changed their names for the sake of anonymity) I would certainly not be who I am or be doing what I am doing right now. Jack was the lead pastor of my home church. He endured thirteen years of meeting in high schools before the church could afford its own building. There were highs, but there were lots of lows as well. There were many days he wondered if he had made the right decision, leaving the comfort of a well-established church for the tough and risky road of church planting. But his obedience paved the way for so many lives to be touched and changed, mine being one of them. I was married in that church, I served under my first ministry assignment there, my husband became a pastor there, I wrote my first Bible study while attending there, and the list goes on and on. Without that church, there is no call to church plant for my husband and me. And we're speaking of just a single life! Just think of the many lives that were transformed and are yet to be transformed through one man's decision to be obedient.

I was the speaker in the church that day. That morning I happened to be preaching was the same morning Sally sensed an urgency to walk through the front doors. I had just finished the first draft of my Bible study and had asked God to guide my next steps because, let's face it, I had no idea what to do next. Sally's boldness to approach me and ask what seemed like an out-of-place question led me to the publisher who would produce my first study.

Our willingness to heed the voice of God ultimately has great and grand repercussions not only in our own lives but in the lives of countless others. This was true for the people I mentioned above, and it's true for the characters of the stories we have studied this week. Let's take some time to examine just how the obedience of these men had a lasting effect on the course of history.

Peter

Look up Luke 5:9–11. What did Jesus tell Peter he would fish for from now on?

How was this truth that Jesus spoke over him manifested? Look up the following Scriptures and write your answers here.

Acts 3:1–9

Acts 5:15

Acts 9:40

Acts 10:34

1 Peter 1:1, 2 Peter 2:1

Peter preached to thousands who then became followers of Jesus. He healed more than could ever be counted, raised Tabitha from the dead, was the first to understand salvation was for the Gentiles as well as the Jews, and wrote two letters that later would become beloved books in the New Testament. He indeed became a fisher of men, and you and I are disciples today because of his obedience.

Noah

We have discussed the vast amount of obedience required of Noah to build a ship on dry land with no precedence of rain. But at work under that narrative is a far more significant theme. The backdrop of the story is one of fracture and disconnect. Remember, it begins with, "Now the earth was corrupt in God's sight and was full of violence . . . for all of the peoples on earth had corrupted their ways" (Genesis 6:11, 12). "What is wrong is that creation has refused to be God's creation, refused to honor God as God. Both the world and God have been denied their real character."[85] This is a serious issue and one that demands a response from the Creator-God. At first, it seems He has thrown in the towel. So desperately frustrated and exasperated by his children's total disregard for Him and for one another that the only solution seems to be total destruction. "I am going to bring floodwaters on the earth to destroy all life under the heavens, every creature that has the breath of life in it"(Genesis 6:17). And yet this definitive statement of judgment is followed very quickly by a *but*. "But I will establish a covenant with you," God announces (Genesis 6:18). Humanity might turn its back on God, but the covenant inaugurated here, and sealed with a rainbow, will prove that God will not turn His back on His people.

Read Genesis 7:20, 21.

What does the Lord decree never to do again?

The flood had affected no change in humankind. But it has affected an irreversible change in God, who now will approach His creation with unlimited patience and forbearance.[86] For thousands of years the pattern would remain the same: with one breath God's people would praise His name and with the next curse it. One day they would obey and follow His commands and the next depart for their own way. As Paul would write, "They exchanged the truth about God for a lie, and worshiped and served created things rather than the Creator" (Romans 1:25). And yet, the story of Noah proves God has forever made up His mind. He is for His children and not against them. In a covenant sealed with the blood of his very own Son, He proves over and over again that "if we are faithless, he remains faithful, for He cannot deny Himself" (2 Timothy 2:13). "The good news is that because of his person, this God acts most fully for himself when he acts for the world he created and loves."[87]

---

85 Walter Brueggemann, *Genesis: Interpretation: A Bible Commentary for Teaching and Preaching* (Presbyterian Publishing Corporation). Kindle Edition.

86 Brueggemann, *Genesis: Interpretation: A Bible Commentary.*

87 Brueggemann, *Genesis: Interpretation: A Bible Commentary.*

And Noah plays a great role in the telling of this great truth. Read Hebrews 11:7. What is Noah an heir of?

Noah accepts what we all must. He accepts the gift we all were made to receive. It's the gift of being set right with God. Not because we have done anything to earn or deserve it, and not because we have held up our end of some bargain, but because God has held up His. God has granted us righteousness, and in doing so named us as His children. All Noah had to do was enter into what God was doing for him and trust it. And all we have to do is enter into what God has done for us and trust it.

You see, Noah's obedience didn't just mean life for himself and his family; it meant life for us too. We still live under that covenant, the one where God

FOR THOUSANDS OF YEARS THE PATTERN WOULD REMAIN THE SAME: WITH ONE BREATH GOD'S PEOPLE WOULD PRAISE HIS NAME AND WITH THE NEXT CURSE IT.

holds unswervingly to his Word whether we hold to ours or not. The ripple effect of his obedience is still being felt and will continue to be experienced for generations and generations to come.

Whether we choose to listen to the voice of God or ignore it, our obedience (or lack of it) has ramifications for us and others. What we choose today affects our tomorrow, and not just ours, but those of many. With the stories of these men in mind, let's take a few moments to journal. Here are some questions to help.

Is there a Peter or Noah in your life, someone whom you credit with either a fresh or deepened understanding of faith in Jesus?

How has the obedience of that individual or individuals affected your choices and decisions? Do you believe your life would be markedly different had they not been obedient to their "I have to"?

Can you begin to see yourself as Peter and Noah? Are there people in your life right now who will be profoundly affected by your obedience or disobedience to your "I have to"?

How does this principle, the ripple effect of your obedience, challenge and encourage you to move forward with your "I have to"?

Let me leave you with this question, from author Mark Batterson, to close our time together this week.

"When did we start believing that God wants to send us to safe places to do easy things? That faithfulness is holding the fort? That playing it safe is safe? That there is any greater privilege than sacrifice? That radical is anything but normal?"[88]

---

88 Mark Batterson, *All In* (Grand Rapids, Mich.: Zondervan, 2013), p. 1.

As we follow Jesus we will encounter, not just once or twice but again and again, an utterly nonsensical "I have to." Our lives may not always make sense to us, and if and when that's the case, we should take heart. In fact, we should rejoice. When the path seems to lead us down uncomfortable lanes toward crazy-town, it can only mean one thing: God's up to *something*.

And I want to be in on it when He moves.

WHEN "I HAVE TO" HURTS

Let's review these questions from week five of our personal study.

Day 1

1. What is Peter's profession? What is Jesus' profession? Why does Jesus telling Peter how to do his job seem a bit strange?

2. Is there something God is calling you to do or believe right now that feels nonsensical? If so, what is it?

3. Have you ever felt like Peter? Perhaps you've worked really hard at something and, in the end, in spite of your best efforts, it just wasn't enough; you came up short. Reflect on that time.

4. Are you experiencing a "because you say so . . . " moment? Can you describe it?

Day 2

1. How large was the ark (use modern-day measurements)?

2. How long would you guesstimate it took to build the ark?

3. Has God called you to something that felt crazy? Where you felt like the laughingstock of your family or friend group?

4. Do any of the promises we covered resonate with you? If so, which ones, and why do you think they spoke to you?

Day 3

1. There are some who might say Joshua's military plan was the worst one ever drafted. How so?

2. Why do you think the commander of the Lord's army tells Joshua to take the ark of the covenant with them?

3. Why is fixing our eyes on Jesus so simple in theory and yet so difficult in practice?

4. What are some practical steps you can take to "fix your eyes on Jesus"?

5. How can you let the encouragement and love of God quiet and displace your doubt and discouragement?

Day 4

1. Have you ever wondered why God, both throughout the Scriptures and in our lives as well, chooses to hand out nonsensical "I have to's"? Can you recall a specific time you've questioned God on this topic? What were the circumstances?

2. How many men did Gideon begin with, and how many did he have at the end when he went into battle?

3. According to the Gideon account, why does God give us nonsensical "I have to's"?

4. In your circumstances right now, can you see why God might be pushing you outside your comfort zone so you will learn to trust Him more?

Day 5

1. How did the obedience of Peter affect future generations, including us?

2. How did the obedience of Noah affect future generations, including us?

3. Is there a Peter or Noah in your life, someone whom you credit with either a fresh or deepened understanding of faith in Jesus?

4. How has the obedience of that individual or individuals affected your choices and decisions? Do you believe your life would be markedly different had they not been obedient to their "I have to"?

Watch Session 6 at Christyfay.com: "The Nonsensical 'I Have To'"

The Setup

B y now you've read the title, so you know this week is about what happens when "I have to" hurts. There's a big part of me that wishes I didn't have to center our last week around the word *hurt*. I wish I could call it "when 'I have to' is wonderfully easy and simple." But if I called it that I would be leaving you with a lie, and for a Bible study author that would just be bad form. So here's the hard and difficult reality that we must face together before we close our journey: there's a distinct possibility your "I have to" is going to hurt. But don't trust my word, trust God's Word. Here's what Jesus says about this matter to his disciples.

> *"If you find the godless world is hating you, remember it got its start hating me. If you lived on the world's terms, the world would love you as one of its own. But since I picked you to live on God's terms and no longer on the world's terms, the world is going to hate you"* (John 15:18, 19, MSG).

When you have an "I have to," it's just another way of saying you're living on God's terms. We learned this last week about Noah, Peter, and Gideon and how their "I have to's" compelled them to do things they never, in their right minds, would have done on their own. In this way, they were living on God's terms. Now, the bad news, as Jesus explained, is that when you've been picked to live on God's terms (I would venture to say we've all been picked; we just haven't all said yes), then the world isn't going to like you much. Jesus uses an even stronger word to describe how the world will feel about you. With Jesus there was no sugarcoating things. They are going to "hate you," Jesus says. So yes, there's no avoiding it when you have an "I have to." There's a good chance it might cause you some discomfort, discord, and even pain.

I wrote in last week's introduction about the Wright brothers, the first men to fly an airplane. Both men were fascinated by and naturally gifted in the understanding of mechanics. Orville (still in high school at the time) opened his own printing press. Having served as an apprentice in a print shop two summers earlier, he had observed enough about the inner workings of the press to create his own through use of a discarded tombstone, a buggy spring, and scrap metal.[89] And so the ability to build something from practically nothing was born. In the spring of 1893 the brothers would open their own small bicycle business, selling and repairing bikes.[90] The business was successful, ultimately leading them to open a street-level shop with enough space on the second floor to begin producing their own bicycles.[91] All this was well and good, but they still ached to

89 David McCulllough, *The Wright Brothers* (New York: Simon and Schuster, 2015), p. 18.

90 Ibid, p. 22.

91 Ibid, p. 25.

find that one thing they had been put on this earth to do. They were on a search for their *ikigai*, on the lookout for their "I have to." It would come, as we all know, in the form of a dream, a dream to fly. On Tuesday, March 30, 1899 Wilbur Wright would draft a letter, one of the most important personal correspondences in history. Addressed to the Smithsonian Institution in Washington, D.C., he would request any and all research on the topic of flight and would boldly claim that he was completely convinced "human flight is possible and practical."[92]

Of course, this week is all about how our "I have to's" can be hard. For the Wright brothers this proved exceptionally true. They built their own glider-kite, having studied and read all they could and, perhaps more importantly, having given themselves to the careful observation of birds in flight.[93] They then made their way to Kitty Hawk, North Carolina, where the winds that whipped off the Atlantic Ocean created the perfect opportunity to test their newly constructed glider. They set up camp, literally sleeping in a large tent, which did very little to shield them from the elements.

> THERE'S A DISTINCT POSSIBILITY YOUR "I HAVE TO" IS GOING TO HURT. BUT DON'T TRUST MY WORD, TRUST GOD'S WORD.

Many nights the wind was such that they had to leap from bed to hold the tent down. "When we crawl out of the tent to fix things, the sand fairly blinds us," Orville wrote. "We each have two blankets, but almost freeze every night."[94]

They were mocked by the locals, who thought these bird-studying loonies trying to take flight themselves had lost their minds. It would take several trips to Kitty Hawk, and all kinds of failures, injuries, and sleepless nights, nearly freezing themselves in the process, and obscene amounts of hours building and rebuilding their gliders before they would finally arrive at the needed solutions. Still, it would be years before anyone would believe that these two unlikely brothers had cracked the seemingly uncrackable code of flight engineering. And all of this was accomplished with very little support and funding. To give some perspective, there were others chasing the same dream. One man was Samuel Langley, whose experimental project had cost $70,000, mostly public money, and had failed entirely. Between 1900 and 1903, including materials and travel to and from Kitty Hawk, the Wright brothers spent a little less than $1,000, all of that coming from the proceeds from their bicycle business.[95]

92 Ibid, p. 32.

93 Ibid, p. 37.

94 Ibid, p. 53.

95 Ibid, p. 108.

The Wright brothers had an "I have to," and it was hard; it cost them something. But it also gave the world an incredible gift. They proved, as they set out to, that "human flight is both possible and practical." I am grateful they didn't give up but instead persevered through the many trials and tribulations.

Our "I have to" very well might hurt as well. So this week let's lean in instead of leaning away. Let's work hard to push through the pain and struggle so we can say, as Timothy wrote, "I have fought the good fight, I have finished the race, I have kept the faith" (2 Timothy 4:7).

WEEK 6

WHEN "I HAVE TO" HURTS

Day 1: A Hard Teaching
John 6:26–60; 6:61–70

My oldest son came home the other day, placed his backpack on the hook, grabbed something out of the pantry to snack on, and then grabbed his math worksheet from his take-home folder. This is the routine in our house. The established ritual is food, homework, then free time. It's a rare occasion that we allow a deviation from this order. So Oliver, obedient first child that he is, grabbed his worksheet, some fruit bits, and got to work. It usually takes him about five minutes to finish his homework. However, on this particular day he sat there laboring over his addition problems. (Mind you, he had to add two sets of three-digit numbers, a problem that requires a calculator for his mom!) It was taking longer than normal. He let out a few strained sighs to indicate his overall frustration with the assignment and also to lure a "you need help, buddy?" from me, which it did.

And yet he responded, "No. This is just really hard."

Have you ever had that kind of experience? Maybe at the gym when your friend, trainer, or instructor forces five extra repetitions on you? Or maybe in the kitchen with a recipe that calls for surplus amounts of effort? Or perhaps you're battling something in your personal life, a broken marriage or a difficult cancer treatment, and all you can

147

think is, *This is so hard.* Whatever comes to your mind, jot it below, no matter how significant or insignificant it seems.

In today's reading we will find the disciples experiencing the same sentiment you did in the experience you journaled about above: "This is hard." Turn to John 6:60 and fill in the following blanks.

On hearing it, _____ of his disciples said, "This is a _____ teaching. Who can accept it?" (John 6:60).

Of course, this statement begs the question, What teaching did Jesus did give that left them feeling defeated and overwhelmed? This is precisely what we will be diving into today. Before we do that, glance back to the beginning of John chapter six. What miracle of Jesus opens this chapter?

Jesus has just fed the crowds, taking five barley loaves and two fish and miraculously multiplying these few scraps to feed the more than five thousand people gathered there that day. As if that wasn't enough, Jesus ups his game later that night by coming to his frightened disciples, their boat nearly capsized by the winds and waves—walking on water! Once the boat has reached the other side of the lake and arrived at the city of Capernaum, the crowds find Jesus again. "When they found him on the other side of the lake, they asked him, 'Rabbi, when did you get here?'" (John 6:26).

Now that we're caught up with the story, we're going to break Jesus' teaching into three sections. The text is layered with all kinds of meaning, but we'll do our best to tackle it one part at a time.

Section 1: There's more going on than what meets the eye
Begin by reading John 6:26–34.
Why does Jesus say the crowd is looking for him (John 6:26)?

Jesus tells the crowds that to do the works God requires, they must believe. What do the crowds want from Jesus so they might believe (John 6:30)?

Who does Jesus say gives the true bread from Heaven (John 6:33)?

The crowd is focused on the physical realm. They ate and were filled by the fish and loaves. Their ancestors ate and were filled by the manna given them by Moses (or, as Jesus reminds them, by God). If they are going to believe, as Jesus asserts they should, then there must be a sign of something physical, something tangible. But Jesus is pressing them to see that there's more going on here than merely what meets the eye. There is a bread available to them that will fill their hunger (and the hunger of the whole world), not just momentarily, but eternally.

Section 2: Jesus is that bread
Read John 6:35–51.

Jesus makes a similar statement on three separate occasions in this section: 6:35, 6:41, and 6:48. What is it?

Why do the crowds grumble in John 6:41?

What is the bread, according to Jesus, in John 6:51?

In this section Jesus clearly explains that the bread He has spoken about, the bread that will provide life sustenance to the crowds forever, is *Himself*. "I am the bread of life," He announces. Just as God sent the manna to Moses, so now God has sent His son to give life to the whole world. Of course, reading this in our day, in view of Jesus' death and resurrection, it all makes perfect sense. Back then, on the other hand . . . well, you might be able to see how the concept would have been a tricky one for his disciples and fellow Jews to wrap their heads around.

Section 3: "Eat my flesh and drink my blood"
Read John 6:52–60.
What does Jesus say we must do to have life (John 6:53)?

What happens when we eat the flesh of Jesus and drink His blood (John 6:56)?

Jesus turns to His disciples and to the crowds gathered to hear Him teach, and what He says next shocks them all: "You must eat of my flesh and drink of my blood." Can you even imagine how strange and outright awkward those words would have sounded? Again, remember this conversation is occurring before Jesus' death and resurrection. Much if not all of this terminology—"eat my flesh, drink my blood"—is lost on His listeners. It would have been nearly impossible to discern its meaning prior to those events. Perhaps this is why the disciples, upon hearing these words, responded with, "This is a hard teaching. Who can accept it?" (John 6:60).

At the heart of Jesus' discourse is the idea that, without Him, we can do nothing. It's only by remaining in Him that we find real and true life. Jesus would later repeat this same sentiment in John 15: "I am the vine and you are the branches. If you remain in me and I in you, you will bear much fruit; *apart from me you can do nothing*" (John 15:5, emphasis added). Here the metaphor is less shocking, so why did Jesus begin teaching about this concept of His indwelling in us by using such vivid and, yes, even offensive imagery as eating flesh and drinking blood? I think it's because there is no clearer example of one life being laid down for the sake of another than in eating and drinking. We can enjoy a juicy hamburger because, somewhere, a cow gave up its life! That wonderful cow laid down his life so I could have the energy I need to sustain my life. N. T. Wright put it this way.

> The eating and the drinking has to do with shared life, mutual indwelling. In the physical realm one of the most powerful examples of shared life is eating and drinking—the laying down of life by a plant or animal and the interpenetration of life as molecules are transferred, thereby nourishing life.[96]

We only find true life by entrusting our lives completely to the Father through the Son, and this only occurs through the indwelling of the Holy Spirit. Although seemingly complex, all that Jesus has just said can be boiled down to the statement I made above.

96 Tom Wright, *John for Everyone Part 1: Chapters 1–10, Part 1* (New Testament for Everyone). SPCK. Kindle Edition, p. 83.

So why is it so offensive to the disciples? Why is it so hard? Why does it cause many of His disciples to turn back and stop following Him (John 6:66)? I will write what I think, but first journal here what *you* think.

What we are faced with once again is the issue of control. Following Jesus means understanding that, apart from Him, we can do nothing. Just repeat that phrase aloud to yourself a few times over. "Apart from Him I can do nothing. Apart from Him I can do nothing. Apart from Him I can do nothing." Is there a voice inside you that rises up and begins to protest, if not forcefully then subtly? It might sound something like this:

JESUS IS PRESSING THEM TO SEE THAT THERE'S MORE GOING ON HERE THAN MERELY WHAT MEETS THE EYE. THERE IS A BREAD AVAILABLE TO THEM THAT WILL FILL THEIR HUNGER.

"I can do it."

"I'm strong, I'm smart, I'm highly educated, I'm unequivocally qualified, and I don't need someone telling me what to do or how to live my life."

"Is there anyone who could really understand me better than me? Is there anyone else who can really know what I want and how to get it other than me?"

If we're honest and genuinely candid with ourselves, these kinds of questions surface, if not at first, then usually over the course of time. We don't like the idea of someone else bossing us around, even if it is exactly what we need. We prefer independence over dependence by nature, and this philosophy is reinforced by our culture.

Yet at the heart of Jesus' teaching is an urging, a relinquishing of control. True life comes only in childlike faith and trust, in total and complete surrender. True life comes to us not through striving and straining but through remaining and resting in One much greater than ourselves. And that, my friends, is hard. And sometimes it hurts.

What about you? Do you find it difficult to trust another with your life? Is control over your circumstances something you crave? Why or why not?

Today has been a marathon lesson, hasn't it? This is indeed a difficult teaching. But I would fail you if I didn't have you read the final verses of this chapter. So bear down; we are almost there. Read the final ten verses, John 6:61–70.

How does our dear friend Peter respond when Jesus turns to his closest disciples and asks, "You do not want to leave too, do you?"

"Lord, to whom shall we go? You have the words of eternal life," Peter replies to Jesus. Because, in the end, this really is the only answer. Following Jesus is hard, and sometimes it hurts. It means trusting, letting go, and remaining instead of striving. The truth is our "I have to's" often force us to these deeper places of surrender, which is precisely why they hurt. So friends, when your "I have to" hurts, take heart, because it's leading you exactly where true life is found, in the safe and secure hold of Jesus. There is no better place to be.

Day 2: The Test
Genesis 22:1–19

I am mother to four young children, so I know all about the struggles every two-year-old and their parents face. One is the hard-fought lesson of sharing. And let me tell you from experience, the struggle is real. Letting a friend or (even harder) a sibling share a little one's toys, clothes, video game, and more is a lot to handle. Usually a form of torture parents place on their children involves a highly desired item (anything from a *Star Wars* lightsaber to a random piece of ribbon found on the floor) and the encouragement to share or hand it over to someone else. The result: all kinds of kicking, screaming, and general tantrum-throwing. Many of us are parents, and we've been there; we are well acquainted with the blood-boiling frustration that rises from within. For adults the solution is so obvious: just release your death grip on the doll and *share it for Pete's sake!*

Now the irony of it all is that when it comes to our own adult lives, we are just as unwilling, if not more so, to release and relinquish control. This is precisely why our "I have to's" can hurt. They often force us to bend our knees and surrender our will to a power much greater than our own. This process of relinquishing the death grip we have on the metaphorical wheel of our lives can be excruciatingly uncomfortable.

Speaking of uncomfortable, today we are going to look at a story that might distress you a bit—at least on first reading it. But don't be discouraged; we are going to tackle this rather disconcerting section of Scripture together, and I believe you will be somewhat surprised and even enlightened by where it leads us. Begin by reading the very first sentence of Genesis 22:1 and fill in the blank.

Some time later God _____ Abraham.

Does that word *tested* make your insides clench up a bit like it did mine? If you're me, that word immediately transports you back to the ninth grade. All of a sudden, my palms begin to sweat, the smell of freshly sharpened pencil fills my nostrils, and I'm sitting at my desk staring at algebra problems I'm not sure how to solve.

What about you: how does this word make you feel?

The truth is, as much as it pains me to say this, tests are necessary. There was no way for my ninth-grade teacher to know whether I could do quadratic equations other than testing me on the specific material. In the same way, our faith must be tested. Read 1 Peter 1:6, 7.

> *In all this you greatly rejoice, though now for a little while you may have had to suffer grief in all kinds of trials. These have come so that the proven genuineness of your faith—of greater worth than gold, which perishes even though refined by fire—may result in praise, glory and honor when Jesus Christ is revealed.*

According to this passage, why do we experience trials or tests?

our sole purpose is to give God glory.

Our "I have to's" hurt from time to time because they often test us, and they press us into deeper places of trust, which in turn reveals the true nature of our faith.

With all that in mind, read the rest of this amazing story, in Genesis 22:1–19.

OK, right now, before you do anything else, journal what you are feeling. Don't hold back, and don't write what you think I or anyone else wants to hear. Whatever this story evokes, raw and real as it might be, write it down.

So you don't feel left out, here's some stream of consciousness thoughts that I had . . .

Hold up. Wait a minute. Did the God who made Abraham wait twenty-plus years for a son really just ask him to sacrifice that same son?

   Did Abraham just really go for it?

   What kind of bloodthirsty God would do that?

   If that's how God is, I'm not sure I want to follow Him.

   If that's what God is like, asking his followers to murder their sons and daughters, then I'm out on this whole thing.

   How could Abraham even entertain the idea of killing his own flesh and blood?

I could keep going, but you get the point. This passage draws out the full spectrum of our emotions, doesn't it? Shock that churns into anger that bubbles into confusion and then back to anger. Let's get to the bottom of all of this, shall we? It begins by wading into the world and culture in which Abraham finds himself and seeking to understand how it influences this story.

In Abraham's world there are plenty of gods. One, it seemed, for everything. Rain, fertility, small animals, thunder—the list goes on, one god assigned to each and every facet of life. At least that's what was believed to be true. Now, let's just imagine that your only source of food comes from the ground you tend with your hands. You've planted tomatoes, lettuce, carrots, a whole garden for that matter, but there is one thing you need for it to grow: water. *I'll pray to the rain god*, you think. *Just maybe he or she will listen and give me what I need.* If the rain comes, you'll know you must have done something right; the god heard your cry or saw all your hard work and responded accordingly. But if it doesn't . . . well then, what do you assume? The rain god must be angry with me. I've done something to irritate him. And the next question you ask, because your livelihood depends on it, is, Is there something I can do to appease him?

CAN'T YOU JUST PICTURE ABRAHAM NOW, HIS SON ISAAC WITH HANDS AND FEET BOUND? THE KNIFE PRECARIOUSLY PERCHED OVER THE SON'S QUIVERING THROAT, ABRAHAM'S EYES BLOODSHOT AND HIS HEART NEARLY ABOUT TO BURST WITH THE ABSOLUTE TERROR.

Now fast-forward twelve months. Any surplus food you had has now been depleted, you're starving, and so is your entire family. You've tried everything you can think of but still not a single drop of rain. You're desperate. You've heard of others who have offered up their very own child to the gods, because really, is there anything of greater value? Perhaps this is what it will take to turn the tide. So, why not? What do you have to lose? You're willing to sacrifice one of your children so that you can save the lives of your other six.

It is excruciatingly difficult to wrap our brains around the idea of child sacrifice. It's a foreign and barbaric practice in our culture. But at the time in which Abraham is living and for years after, this was the norm. If you wanted something bad enough, you would do whatever it took to get the attention of the gods, to get them on your side, to satisfy their bloodlust. So when God comes to Abraham and says,

"Take your son, your only son, whom you love—Isaac—and go to the region of Moriah. Sacrifice him there as a burnt offering on a mountain I will show you" (Genesis 22:2).

. . . Well, this might not even have been so much of a shock to Abraham. This just further proves the point that this God is just like all the other gods, doesn't it?[97] Or is He?

We read this story though our twenty-first century lens and are shocked by a God who would demand the sacrifice of a firstborn son. How crass, how crude, how utterly barbaric, we think. But this does not surprise Abraham. No, the surprise for Abraham comes when God says, "Wait, stop. Do not touch even one hair on his head." Can't you just picture Abraham now, his son Isaac with hands and feet bound? The knife precariously perched over the son's quivering throat, Abraham's eyes bloodshot and his heart nearly about to burst with the absolute terror of the inhumane and horrific task before him. But in an instant, everything changes. He hears the familiar voice of his God calling his name: "Abraham! Abraham!" He has suspected that God might intervene all along, but now there is viable proof. This God is different from the rest. Those other gods may demand the sacrifice of your firstborn, but this God does not.

In this dramatic narrative God has clearly made his point; He has set Himself apart from the rest. And yet, there's still a question to be wrestled with. Was this really the only way to test Abraham's allegiance? Wasn't there another way, far less traumatic, a way lacking a treasured only son and a knife? Why do you think God still had Abraham walk out this test in this way? There are no right or wrong answers in tackling this question. Just journal whatever you think.

Our "I have to's" often force us to come face to face with our truest intentions and motivations. We have a tendency to think that our "I have to's" are for the world out there. *Someone out there needs me to swoop in on my white horse and, in superhero-like fashion, save the day.* Or so we think. We think the reason God mandates "I have to's" is for the person over there who desperately needs us. And there is some truth to that. At the end of last week's study we traced how our obedience has a ripple effect for generations to come. But we would be wrong if we believed the lie that God cares more about the outcome of our obedience than our obedience itself. He is far more concerned with the state of our hearts than he is with our saving the world. What does Proverbs 4:23 say we should do with our hearts?

97 Rob Bell, *The Gods Aren't Angry* (Zondervan, 2008). DVD.

There is no way to pollute our "I have to" more than by ignoring the condition of our hearts. God, as the supreme guardian, places tests in our lives for two reasons.

One: that we might have greater insight into the character of God Himself. Two: that we might have greater insight into our own character.

In this story Abraham learns that he has assumed a few things about God that just aren't true. This God isn't like the others. But he also has realized a few things about himself. He has been tested and his faith proven true. In the midst of death, literal death, he believes that His God will find a way. When his son asks him where the lamb for the offering is, Abraham responds, "God himself will provide the lamb" (Genesis 22:8). There seems to be no way out, but in his heart Abraham trusts that His God will find a way. He has believed what Jesus would press his disciples to believe in the passage we read yesterday. God is the only author of life, and He alone has the power to give it, sustain it, or take it away. And He is a God of resurrection as well! In our lowest and most desperate moments, the ones in which we believed there was no overcoming, God proves otherwise. As Walter Brueggemann wrote:

> Resurrection concerns the keeping of a promise when there is no ground for it. Faith is nothing other than trust in the power of the resurrection against every deathly circumstance. Abraham knows beyond understanding that God will find a way to bring life even in this scenario of death.[98]

Abraham trusts God. With everything that's worth anything on the line, he believes. That faith is what allows him to see God for who He really is. Not just another angry god who demands the sacrifice of a firstborn son. Abraham's "I have to" hurts, but it also opens his eyes to see the true character of himself and of God.

As we close, I would love for you to ask a few important questions. Journal your reflections.

What kinds of misconceptions do you have about God?

---

98 Walter Brueggemann, *Genesis: Interpretation: A Bible Commentary for Teaching and Preaching* (Presbyterian Publishing Corporation). Kindle Edition.

It it possible that your culture, your upbringing, or your previous church experience has tainted your perception of God? If so, how?

What is the specific lie you are believing about the character of God? What is the truth about who He is?

Do you believe, as Abraham did, that in your darkest days God will provide what you need? What does resurrection look like and mean to you?

Dear friends, it is so easy to allow past hurts, circumstances, and people to shape how we view God. The truth is, although Christians are called to be the living embodiment of Christ, we often fail miserably, leaving collateral damage in the wake. But, I beg you, even though it might be exceptionally difficult and painful, allow God to reshape and redefine your view of Himself. I'm praying for you as you open yourself to this work of God in your life.

Day 3: Blind Spots
Luke 18:18–29

Yesterday we looked at how our "I have to's" can lead us to hard places. For Abraham, it was to the altar with his only and dearest son Isaac, a knife, and an impossible task. This unbearably painful "I have to" led Abraham to the understanding that his God was unlike the other gods. Abraham's "I have to" forced him to wrestle with his misconceptions and misinterpretations of God. In the end, he found a way to trust God to provide a way out, and God, in keeping with His character, did just that. "Abraham looked up and there in the thicket he saw a ram caught by its horn" (Genesis 22:13). His son was not to be the sacrifice. It would be the ram instead.

We also learned from our previous lesson that God cares more about the condition of our hearts than the condition of our "I have to's." Today's story will serve to further reinforce that point. Sometimes our "I have to's" press us to wrestle with our misconceptions of God, and sometimes our "I have to's" press us to wrestle with our misconceptions about ourselves. Today we will tackle the latter.

Now let's read Luke 18:18–29.

What question does the ruler ask Jesus in Luke 18:18?

At first glance this question seems innocent enough. This man simply wants to know what he must do to inherit eternal life . . . or does he? This question is harmless if its intent is grounded in pure and genuine curiosity, but I don't believe it is. If we read between the lines a little bit (and Jesus' response helps us do this), we can see this question is more rhetorical in nature. When the man asks, "Good teacher, what must I do to inherit eternal life?" what he's really saying is, "Good teacher, I've kept all the commands my whole life, so I'm going to inherit eternal life, right?" The question mark is optional, actually, because, in the man's mind, he's gone and earned his "eternal life badge" due to his faithfulness to the law.

Of course, Jesus immediately sees through this man's garbage and, to put it frankly, he sees through ours too. In a sense Jesus calls the young man's bluff. Fill in the blank below from Luke 18:22.

When Jesus heard this, he said to him, "You still _____ one thing."

This one brief statement spoken by Jesus turns the man's life completely upside down. Until this moment there hasn't been even a thought in the man's mind that he might lack something. If we could listen to the young ruler's inner dialogue, here's how I think it would go:

"Lack," what are you talking about, "lack"? I've kept every command; I've done it all right, I've got this whole thing worked out to perfection. Can't you see I'm winning at life? Me? Yeah, I don't lack anything.

And this is precisely the problem. When we show up to a conversation, a relationship, or an opportunity believing that we lack nothing, it often means we will walk away sad, just like this man did. His is not a posture of humility. He is looking not to learn from Jesus but instead for Jesus to affirm his goodness. The rich young ruler is both surprised and troubled when Jesus uses this interaction to point out an area of lacking in his life.

What does Proverbs 16:18 name the attitude and posture that the man is inhabiting in this story?

Pride. A five-letter word that is at the root of so much of our trouble. C. S. Lewis, one of the greatest theologians and thinkers of our time, wrote, "For pride is spiritual cancer: it eats up the very possibility of love, or contentment, or even common sense."[99] Common sense is precisely what this rich young ruler is missing when he stands before the Son of God and claims he, in and of himself, has earned eternal life on his own merit.

Pride rears its ugly head in our lives as well, and the outcome is far from endearing. Pride tells us the story that our ways, thoughts, and actions are in some way better than those around us. It weaves the lie into our hearts that we are competent in and of ourselves to do what, in reality, only God can do. It seeks to gain sole credit for our successes and to deny responsibility for our shortcomings. It isn't pretty, that's for sure.

You know that space in your car's side mirrors, the ones commonly referred to as a blind spot? It's that one place that gives the driver the illusion there is no car to the back left or back right when, in reality, there may be. Recently, engineers who design and manufacture cars have gotten smart and added extra mirrors or cameras to eliminate the blind spot, therefore decreasing the number of accidents. I don't have any statistics to prove whether their efforts have actually brought greater safety to our roads, but what I do know is we have blind spots too. Our blind spots are born from pride and can manifest themselves in various forms and functions in our lives.

Sometimes it looks like an addiction we aren't willing to name, or a mouth we can't seem to keep from spewing all kinds of negativity. Sometimes it's a toxic relationship we swear isn't causing us any harm or a deep-seated need to always have the best and newest thing. It can look like all kinds of things, but it's our pride that feeds it.

99 C. S. Lewis, *Mere Christianity* (Harper Collins: New York, 2001).

So, what is the rich young ruler's blind spot (Luke 18:22, 23)?

Our blind spots can be quite dangerous, especially if we aren't aware they exist. That's why one of the first rules of driving is to check your side and rearview mirrors and to glance backward and sideways before making a lane change. If you know there's a blind spot, then you can take the right precautions.

Dear friends, we must familiarize ourselves with our personal blind spots, and it starts by admitting we have them. It begins with us saying, "I know that I'm lacking, that I'm broken, and that I don't have it all together. I know I am weak and in need of something I simply cannot attain to on my own or provide for by myself." This is the birthplace of humility, and it's the only viable defense to pride. So how can we know our blind spot when the name, in and of itself, communicates we are blind to it? As most things do, it begins with prayer.

Read Psalm 139:23. I've provided it for you here. Circle the words and underline the phrase(s) that stand out to you.

Search me, God, and know my heart; test me and know my anxious thoughts (Psalm 139:23).

Isn't it interesting that what David is asking God to do is test him? Much like Abraham, David wants to understand where his misconceptions of himself, others, and God lie. Asking God to search us in this way is the only path to true transformation.

Now, take a moment and be still before God. Read this short verse from the Psalms several times over. Is there something that comes to your mind? You may already be aware of a blind spot in your life, and God is bringing it to the surface again, or you may sense God sifting something out that He hasn't been able to before. Whatever it is, write it in the space here.

Our "I have to's" will often force us to come face to face with our greatest weakness and our deepest places of lacking. When God sheds lights on our blind spots, we are confronted with a choice. Will I respond with pride and ignore them? Or will I respond in humility and seek greater understanding and insight? We do not have to be like the rich young ruler, who refused to step into the healing and wholeness Jesus was offering. We do not have to turn away saddened but instead can accept the life-giving challenge God is presenting before us, and follow Him.

There is something altogether miraculous that happens when we own up to our weakness. In his letter to the church at Corinth, what does Paul say happens? Read 2 Corinthians 12:9.

When we finally come to terms with our own lacking and insufficiencies and surrender them to God, He uses them to most strongly reflect His glory. It's in those moments when we are mostly acutely aware of our need that He can do the most work both in and through us.

If you are addicted to alcohol and finally arrive at your moment of acceptance, you will find, in due time, and after healing in your life, that you will be used to help another find freedom in theirs. You might find that once you confess your words that often inflict harm instead of bringing about healing, God will begin a work of transformation in and through you. And perhaps one day others will name you as one of their greatest champions and encouragers. Then you will see that what once was your greatest area of weakness . . . God will now use to most profoundly display His strength, glory, and might.

SO HOW CAN WE KNOW OUR BLIND SPOT WHEN THE NAME, IN AND OF ITSELF, COMMUNICATES WE ARE BLIND TO IT? AS MOST THINGS DO, IT BEGINS WITH PRAYER.

Of course, these things cannot and will not happen unless our eyes are opened to what we were blind to see. And they certainly will not happen through our own wisdom and strength. It's only by leaning in and embracing the power of the Almighty that we can face our insufficiencies and flaws and find that they have become portraits of His hand of healing in our life.

Day 4: Glimpsing the Glory
2 Chronicles 2:1, 2; 7:1–3

One night my husband and I were out with a large group of friends for a surprise birthday party. I happened to sit next to a girlfriend of mine. We will call her Anne for the sake of anonymity. Anne and I began chatting about our children. She has two young sons; one was three and the other just a few months old at this point. "It's been so hard lately," she began and, without further explanation, I knew she was talking about this particular point in her mothering career. Her oldest had breached those difficult toddler years. They call it the "terrible twos," but in my experience the terrible twos extend well into the threes and fours. "It seems like he's always pushing the limits," Anne said. "Every moment for him is an opportunity to test me, and all I feel like I do is say no." She sighed heavily. "I just don't know how you do it with four."

She and her husband had been married for ten years before they decided to begin their family. Before motherhood she had been very successful in her career and climbed to the top of the corporate ladder in her field. As we talked, it became clear that what was especially challenging about her fairly new role as a full-time mom was the lack of recognition. In her career there had been promotions, deals made, commissions, and much more that made her feel as though her role was vital to the success of the company. Her job provided her with crystal-clear purpose. She was valued by her boss and associates, and most days there was clear evidence that what she was doing was making an impact. On top of that, every few weeks there was a paycheck, more decisive proof that what she was doing with her time was valuable, not just to her company but also to her personal bank account.

When she traded her briefcase for bottles and her heels for a house robe, she was faced with the sobering reality that no one cares or applauds you for being able to pick up a soother with your toes or make baby food from scratch. There is a steady stream of snotty noses and poopy bottoms to wipe, ungodly amounts of laundry, and no one to hand you an award when you get both your kids to nap at the same time, although an award is exactly what you deserve. You can't even get your husband to affirm you on the nights—OK, night—you manage to get dinner on the table having also kept the children alive for the entire day. He remarks that the green beans are soggy and the chicken overcooked, and you want to reach across the table and strangle him with your bare hands.

Mothering is, hands-down, one of greatest "I have to's" I have ever received. But it also one of the hardest. Why? Because most days you feel utterly alone, highly undervalued, and unbelievably exhausted. It is a tireless and thankless job. One day our children will, we hope, recognize the fruits of our efforts and thank us profusely (no wait, maybe

I'm going too far there!). Anyway, until then we will soldier on with very little fanfare and on most days without much gratitude. Don't get me wrong. Being a mother has handed me some of the greatest joys I've experienced here on planet earth, but it is not for the faint of heart.

Our "I have to's" are hard because sometimes they leave us feeling undervalued, underappreciated, and convinced that our efforts are in vain.

Now read 2 Chronicles 2:1, 2.

David had hoped he would be the one chosen to build a temple for the Lord, but it was his son Solomon who God had assigned to this "I have to." It was no small task, one that Solomon would never dream of taking on himself.

Do some quick math: how many men did Solomon employ to build the temple? (Add the number of carriers plus the number of stonecutters and the number of foremen and you have a start.)

Since we are in math mode, take a moment and estimate how long you think it took to build the entire temple? (No pressure here; just wager a guess.)

It took 180,600 men to build the temple, and it took them seven years to complete it.[100] Just think of the tediousness of that task. Brick by brick, stone by stone, all done by hand, with limited technology and no machinery or computers to assist. I wonder if there were days these men wondered if what they were doing actually mattered. On day one hundred and three in year two, for instance, did they think to themselves, *Will this work ever end? Will anyone ever take notice of me and the backbreaking labor I have endured for the sake of this great temple?* Maybe there were moments where they felt defeated and flat-out "over it." It's entirely possible I'm just filtering this story through my modern-day millennial lens; perhaps their culture didn't obsess about finding fulfillment and uncovering meaning in their work like we do. Maybe they didn't care that they would remain nameless, just one of hundreds of thousands, never credited or applauded for their work.

If we're honest, we need to know that our work matters. And I think most of us, at least from time to time, question whether it does. We look around and wonder, Does anyone see me? In the middle of the night, when I'm nursing my infant or when it's three hours past quitting time and I'm still at the office, does anyone even notice? Or perhaps even more so, does anyone even care? Are the blood, sweat, and tears I've shed over my "I have to" worth it in the end? When work gets tedious, when the hours are long, when

---

100 John Bowker, *The Complete Bible Handbook* (New York: D.K. Publishing, 1998), p. 133.

the days and years pass by with seemingly very little progress made, our "I have to's" get hard, very hard.

Can you identify with how the workers responsible for the construction of the temple might have felt? Share your thoughts.

Do you sometimes question the meaning of your work? How so?

We are going to fast-forward in the story a bit for our next reading. Now turn to 2 Chronicles chapter 7 and read the first three verses. The time has finally come, the endless hours of excruciating backbreaking labor over, days that stretched into months and then years—it all comes to a head in this moment. The temple in all of its majesty and beauty is being revealed and dedicated to the Lord.

As Solomon finishes his prayer, what happens?

What do the Israelites do in response to the glory of God filling the temple?

The "glory of God": it's a strange and somewhat unfamiliar concept for us today, isn't it? By definition, when the word *glory* is used in relation to God, it "represents a quality corresponding to Him and by which He is recognized."[101] The glory of God makes us witness to the true nature of His character. In more ways than not, God is a mystery. He cannot be grasped or held or seen, at least in the physical realm. But when His glory appears, what's revealed is a glimpse of God as He truly is, not as we have imagined Him to be. Of course, it's merely a glimpse. The promise we have, as recorded by Paul, is that

101 James Strong, LLD, STD, *Strong's Expanded Exhaustive Concordance of the Bible* (Nashville: Thomas Nelson Publications, 2010), p. 3519.

one day we will know God as He fully knows us. "For now we see only a reflection as in a mirror; then we shall see face to face. Now I know in part; then I shall know fully, even as I am fully known" (1 Corinthians 13:12). Until then, we peek at God as a reflection in the mirror; the mirror is otherwise known as His glory.

Look at 2 Chronicles 7:3. As the Israelites bow in worship, prostrate before Him, with their faces to the ground, what part of His character is revealed?

This God, as revealed to them by His glory, which fills the temple, is good and loving. His love is the kind that endures forever.

Read 1 Corinthians 6:19, 20 and fill in the following blanks.

Do you not know that your bodies are _____ of the Holy Spirit, who is in you, whom you have received from God? You are not your own; you were bought at a price. Therefore _____ God with your bodies (1 Corinthians 6:19, 20).

During the time in which Solomon ruled, the temple was the center of worship, the place where God's glory resided. "Solomon's temple was the center of the national religion of the Judeans, although it was not perhaps the only temple to Yahweh. Its presence in the capitol Jerusalem signified the actual presence of God among the people, and it became for them a powerful symbol."[102]

Modern-day followers of Yahweh don't flock to the temple to worship because they themselves have become a temple where the presence of God resides. Yes, many of us attend some kind of church, but church is far less about walls and much more so about people. Gathering together merely serves to reminds us that we are image bearers, marked and sealed by the Spirit of God. In the context of our spiritual communities we find that same Spirit at work in the lives of those around us, and we are mutually encouraged by the image of God in one another.

> **THE GLORY OF GOD MAKES US WITNESS TO THE TRUE NATURE OF HIS CHARACTER. IN MORE WAYS THAN NOT, GOD IS A MYSTERY.**

In a sense, we become a house where the glory of God can dwell. We have an opportunity every day to reveal the true nature of His character through the power of His Spirit who dwells in us. For those around us who have failed to see God, for whom He remains a mystery, veiled and unknown, we become glimpses of glory.

102 Bowker, *The Complete Bible Handbook*, p. 133.

No one has ever seen God; but if we love one another, God lives in us and his love is made complete in us (1 John 4:12).

Our "I have to's" can be hard because we often never know how God has used our work to become a "glimpse of glory" for someone else. I sure hope that all of those men, the laborers and foremen, got to be there that day as the Israelites gathered together and Solomon dedicated the temple. I sure hope they too got to bow down as the glory of God filled the temple and echoes of His mercy and enduring love were revealed. And I hope they knew, at least in that moment, that the hours of tedious bricklaying were what made it all possible.

Today, whatever it is you face, I pray you're reminded that you are God's temple. That your work—as a mother, a pastor, a teacher, an accountant, a wedding planner, an artist, a whatever it is—it all matters. It matters because you are God's ambassador, His representative in the world. That you, in and of yourself, are home to God's glory. There is at least one person, and more likely many more, who will understand who God is because of your life's work. May that knowledge give you strength to carry on no matter how rocky the terrain or how steep the hill.

Day 5: Remember
Deuteronomy 8:2, 10–14

Well, we've arrived at our final day of study together. This, for me, is a bittersweet moment. The process of writing this study, of encountering the Spirit of the living God in and through the page, is no doubt part of my "I have to." And as you already know, or are about to find out, there is nothing more exhilarating and life-giving than heeding the call and chasing what sets your soul on fire. So, I'm sad to have reached our final day, but I'm also excited because I know that for a fact God has spoken to you in some way. I know this because God has promised through the prophet Isaiah, "As the rain and the snow come down from heaven and do not return without watering the earth and making it bud and flourish, so that it yields seed for the sower and bread for the eater, so is my word that goes out from my mouth; it will not return to me empty, but will accomplish what I desire and purpose for which I sent it" (Isaiah 55:10, 11). So you can rest assured, if you've heard from God through His Word in some way over the last six weeks, if He was woven a dream into your heart and placed an "I have to" in your path, that this is only the beginning. You can be "confident of this, that He who began a good work in you will carry it on to completion" (Philippians 1:6). And if there's still some small part of you that's doubting the truth of this statement, don't. Because that is yet another promise that comes directly from His Word! Isn't it incredible that we serve a God who is able to do immeasurably more than we could even ask or imagine? (See Ephesians 3:20.) Just think of all the adventures He has stirred in your heart over the last few weeks. The plans He has for you makes my heart want to explode with joy and excitement.

But now, back to reality. How do I end this thing? Nearing the end, I feel a bit like a parent, standing in the doorway of their child's dorm room, desperately trying to shove eighteen years of advice and wisdom into one short good-bye. I feel the need to tie up everything God has said and done in the last six weeks with a bright red bow, and yet I feel like I've run out of ribbon, or in this case, I feel like I've run out of the right words. But as I begged God for the right things to write, anything at all that would be His way to end it and not mine—because it's only any good if it comes from Him—there was one word that hit me. One word that seemed to slip from His heart and tuck safely into mine: Remember.

Remember.

You see, we've just spent the last four days talking about how, sometimes, more often than we'd like, our "I have to's" are hard. They push us to deeper places of trust in Him, they force us to wrestle with our misconceptions of God and ourselves, and they challenge us to redefine how we view success and failure. And the truth of the matter is we often make our "I have to's" harder than they . . . have to be. How? Well, that answer is simple: forgetfulness. In our human condition, we are prone to forget. Not only where we last set our keys or put down our sunglasses—although those things too—but we all too quickly forget our God, and more specifically, how our God has never forgotten us.

There's proof of it all over the Scriptures. God does not forget. Complete these Scriptures to get a clearer understanding.

But God _____ Noah and all the beasts and all the cattle that were with him in the ark; and God caused a wind to pass over the earth, and the water subsided (Genesis 8:1).

Then God _____ Rachel, and God gave heed to her and opened her womb (Genesis 30:22).

Then they arose early in the early in the morning and worshipped before the Lord, and returned again to their house in Ramah, and Elkanah had relations with Hannah his wife, and the Lord _____ her (1 Samuel 1:19).

Now it came about in the course of those many days that the king of Egypt died. And the sons of Israel sighed because of the bondage, and they cried out; and their cry for help because of their bondage rose up to God. So God heard their groaning; and God _____ His covenant with Abraham, Isaac, and Jacob. God saw the sons of Israel, and God took notice of them (Exodus 2:23-25).

"Can a woman forget her nursing child [a]nd have no compassion on the son of her womb? Even these may forget, but I will not _____ you. Behold, I have inscribed you on the palms of My hands; Your walls are continually before Me" (Isaiah 49:15, 16).

No, God does not forget us. We are never far from His thoughts or from His heart. But me, on the other hand? I seem to have amnesia, the type where I forget about the far-too-numerous-to-count acts of God's faithfulness. This form of amnesia is usually triggered when fear enters the picture. When I find myself in unknown territory, unsure of the terrain beneath my feet, when my destination is too far to spot up ahead by the naked eye, so far that I forget I've been here before. Not at this exact spot in these same exact circumstances, of course, but in a space just like this one, feeling all the same emotions now that were coursing through my veins then. I forget that the last time I was here, feeling just as apprehensive and fretful as I do now, God made a way where there was no way. That just at the right time a phone call came in, or a check showed up in the mail, or one person said just the right thing at the right moment. I forget that God was *there*, holding my hand, picking me up, whispering words of encouragement in my ear, crying with me, rejoicing over me, and doing every single other thing under the sun I needed most. Of course, I've forgotten, and now I stand frozen in fear, my feet stuck in place. But what power remembering would have if we just did it! What courage it would ignite in my soul! If only I could remember.

What does the Lord say to the Israelites in Deuteronomy 8:2, 10–14?

Remember. Do not forget what I have done, where I have led you, how I have saved you, not just once, but over and over again. Remember how you were oppressed and suffering greatly under the hand of the Egyptians, how I pulled you out and saved you from slavery? Remember the land I promised your ancestor Abraham his descendants would one day occupy, a land flowing with milk and honey, the land I am right now leading you to inhabit? Remember?

What did Jesus say to his disciples as they gathered together for the Last Supper the night he is arrested? Read Luke 22:19.

It is as though Jesus says to us today: "From now on do this, the drinking of the cup and the breaking of bread, in remembrance of me. Remember how I laid down my life so that you could have life. Remember how it was my body that was broken and my blood poured out so you might understand the fullness of the Father's love for you? Remember?"

There is no better way to close our time together than to remember. Not only what He's done in this study, although I hope you'll take a moment to remember that. But to count and treasure and remember *all* the ways he has remembered you.

Let's make a vow to keep track of the thousands of ways He has not forgotten us. As the Psalmist wrote, "I'll write the book on your righteousness, talk up your salvation the livelong day, never run out of good things to write or say. I come in the power of the Lord God, I post signs marking his right-of-way. You got me when I was an unformed youth, God, and taught me everything I know. Now I'm telling the world your wonders; I'll keep at it until I'm old and gray. God, don't walk off and leave me until I get out the news of your strong right arm to this world, news of your power to the world yet to come, your famous and righteous ways, O God. God, you've done ti all! Who is quite like you? (Psalm 71:15–19. MSG). So may I be so bold as to ask you a few more questions before we part?

Remember the "I have to" that God has birthed in your heart through this study. Write about it below.

As you move froward with your "I have to," take a few moments and remember all the ways God has remembered you. List what comes to mind here.

Oh friends, we are now truly at the end. Allow me to speak a blessing and benediction over you: Remember that it is in Christ that we find out who we are and what we are living for. So lean in, listen closely, and boldly live out the "I have to" He places before you.

Now to him who is able to do immeasurably more than all we ask or imagine, according to his power that is at work within us, to him be glory in the church and in Christ Jesus throughout all generations, for ever and ever! Amen (Ephesians 3:20, 21).

Let's review these questions from week six of our personal study.

Day 1

1. Are you experiencing something hard right now? What is it? Review your personal study.

2. What are the crowds looking for from Jesus so that they might believe (John 6:33)?

3. What is the bread of life according to Jesus in John 6:51?

4. What happens when we eat the flesh of Jesus and drink His blood (John 6:56)?

5. Why is this teaching from John 6 considered a "hard teaching" by the disciples?

6. Do you find it difficult to trust another person with your life? Is control over your circumstances something you crave? Why or why not?

Day 2

1. How does the word "test" make you feel? What emotions rise to the surface when you hear the word?

2. When we come to understand the cultural backdrop for the story of Abraham sacrificing Isaac, does it make a little more sense? What was God trying to reveal to Abraham through this seemingly brutal request?

3. What does God care about more than the perfect execution of our "I have to's"?

4. What kind of misconceptions do you have about the character of God?

5. Do you believe, as Abraham did, that in your darkest days God will provide what you need? What does resurrection look like and mean to you?

Day 3

1. What question does the rich young ruler ask Jesus in Luke 18:18?

What does pride do to us? Have you seen its effect in your life? What is that effect?

2. What is the young ruler's blind spot?

3. Have you experienced blind spots when it comes to your character? Have you sensed God bringing those blind spots to light?

4. How have you seen God's strength manifested in and through your weakness?

Day 4

1. Has an "I have to" ever left you feeling exhausted and wondering if your efforts have all been in vain?

2. How many men built the temple under Solomon? How long did it take them?

3. Do you sometimes question the meaning and value of your work?

4. How can our lives become a "glimpse of God's glory"? Have you ever witnessed the character of God in and through the life of someone else? Can you describe what you saw?

Day 5

1. What "I have to" has God brought to the surface for you in the last six weeks?

2. How has God remembered you?

3. How can remembering how God has remembered you give you courage to face your "I have to"?

Watch Session 7 at Christyfay.com: When "I Have to" Hurts